Praise for

Your Greater is Right Now:

Your Greater is Right Now is a relevant word for the world today. Dr. Love provides God's word, practical application activities that lead all walks of life to their greater. This book will help you define and reshape your outlook towards living a greater dependency on God to achieve your purpose.

Pastor Timothy Richardson
Father House Ministries

Your Greater is Right Now is right on time and what people need regardless of where they are at in life. Dr. Derrick Love takes the reader on a personal transparent journey towards living a greater life in a Christ Jesus. Using scripture, real life examples, and personal application ***Your Greater is Right Now*** is both informative and a guide that will lead you to a greater life. I highly recommend this book to anyone who is tired of living a life of mediocrity and ready for greatness now.

Kenneth M. Chapman Jr., Ph.D
Education Administrator
Associate Pastor

This book will change lives. Dr. Love has been vulnerable in his personal walk, with the goal of being a Spirit-led liberating force in the lives of others in pursuit of their Greater. As you read ***Your Greater is Right Now*** prepare to be challenged, encouraged, and released to at last achieve YOUR Greater – God's Greater for your life! Reading this book will release you from the prison of past failures and past limiting thinking and free you to soar at the God-honoring altitudes He has set for Your Greater and His Glory... RIGHT NOW!

Senior Pastor Dono W. Pelham
Life-Changing Faith Christian Fellowship
Frisco, Texas

Your Greater is Right Now/Love is an excellent book for those who are wondering about this season of uncertainty during the midst of COVID-19 Pandemic and the racial current climate.! An indisputable fact we must all remember is that life presents us with hardships and unpredictable timelines. These disruptions from your everyday tend to devalue your faith and confidence in humanity, nature, and God. If you are losing hope due to the world-wide occurrences, this book is for you! This book will provide information and best practices on discovering the greatness within yourself. The book will assist individuals with moving from negative thought process to a positive one helping you to secure a new mental design, an inner construct that is rooted in God's Word that declares who you are. After reading this book, you will embrace the following message and mind set:

- The truth is the Word of God. Other things are mere facts.
- Whatever the Word of God calls you is not a suggestion but the truth.
- God is bound by His Word, and he cannot lie.
- Â So quit seeking approval from social media or from friends.

My favorite part of the book is the section titled, **You Need a Better Reflection. I resonated with this section because it reminds me** you have to come to a place where you become aware of the pictures that are painted in your mind because they'll eventually become templates for your future. What you see is what you become. Fortunately, you do not need to live under the shadows of someone else's achievement or greatness. Likewise, you do not have to be haunted by the negativity that has been spelled out against you by people you have trusted, loved, and respected. Everyone deserves a better and brighter reflection, which can only be found in God, our heavenly Father. THIS IS SO PROFOUND to ENHANCE INNER LOVE FOR OURSELVES!

I strongly recommend this book for those who want to make a personal commitment to define or redefine their greatness as well as release your mind from every limitation. If you want to live your life free of mediocre thought and words, and want to see, think, and speak greatness from now on, **read this book!**

Dr. Greta A Peay, *Chief Executive Officer and Founder*
Infinity: Diversity Matters, LLC
Retried School District Executive administrator

It is with great pleasure, admiration and affinity that I have the opportunity to have been chosen to endorse such a Wonderful and Inspiring book!! Let me begin the endorsement by referencing the fact that I have known Dr. Love for more than 20 years and had the distinct pleasure of being his Pastor for more than 5 years. Dr. Love was an integral part of our youth department serving as Youth Director, Counselor and Motivator of young people in general. The bonds of our relationship have remained strong throughout the years. With that being said, I found the book most helpful to me in that it caused me to do a Self-Examination and really ask myself, "have I achieved all of the greatness assigned to me"? Chapters 1 and 5 really ministered to me as I truly believe we were all "Designed for Greatness"! God in his creativity instilled in us that same ability to be great, we simply have to tap into it! Chapter 5 as well ministered to me as well as I believe our greatness is tied to our Relationship with Christ! Paul said it best, "any man who is in Christ is a new creature, old things have passed away, behold all things have become new"! Your greatness is tied to your faith in Christ! Thank you, Dr. Love, for helping us to realize and achieve our God given greatness. I believe this book will help countless people discover and realize that ***Your Greater Is Right Now***!!

Pastor Patrick L. Turner
Mt. Moriah Missionary Baptist Church
1401 Meadowlane Terrace
Ft. Worth, Tx. 76112

Your Greater is Right Now:

(2nd Edition)

Living as God's
masterpiece instead of
life's middle class

Dr. Derrick Love

Published by Kharis Publishing, imprint of Kharis Media LLC.

ISBN-13: 978-1-63746-120-4
ISBN-10: 1-63746-120-8

Library of Congress Control Number: 2022934169

All KHARIS PUBLISHING products are available at special quantity discounts for bulk purchase for sales, promotions, premiums, fund-raising, and educational needs. For details, contact:

Kharis Media LLC
Tel: 1-479-599-8657
support@kharispublishing.com
www.kharispublishing.com

CONTENTS

Introduction

Greater is he that is in you, than he that is in the world.

1 JOHN 4:4 (KJV)

Everyone has equal potential to be great. Greatness is not limited to some people and removed from the path of others. Greatness is not synonymous with culture, tribe, race, or nationality. Greatness is defined as an individual's inner will to achieve success. In his play *Twelfth Night*, playwright William Shakespeare wrote, "Some are born great, some achieve greatness, and some have greatness thrust upon them."[1] The bottom line? Everyone has the potential to be great.

One notable biblical character that comes to mind who exemplifies greatness is a man by the name of Job. He endured great pain of losing wealth, family, and everything. Job made a conscious decision to trust and believe in God no matter what his situation or circumstance revealed. He fought every step of the way and, in the end, achieved more than he originally had or lost.

Your situation or circumstance does not define you. We may not all achieve greatness in the same way or at the same time, but the good news is that we all have greatness inside of us.

As you read this book, you may be in the darkest corner you have experienced, and you may have listened for God's voice and heard nothing, but the truth is that you can be great. This book will serve as a source of strength for anyone new to the Christian faith, deeper reflection moments for the mature Christian, and hope for anyone looking to move beyond limitations to reach **their greater**. Throughout this book, you will connect, reflect, journal, and even cry as you take steps to identify your passion, purpose, and greatness.

One of the most defining moments for me, which permitted the words of this book, was when I decided to release

---

[1] https://yourstory.com/2017/04/timeless-quotes-william-shakespeare

fear, doubt, resentment, and a host of insecurities. I am a father, husband, an associate pastor for over fifteen years, and a career educator for over eighteen years serving in diverse roles; administrator, teacher, and writer, to name a few. I found myself grappling with the thoughts of feeling not enough, desperation, and a lack of hope within myself. I had achieved great success in my life while feeling depressed and lonely simultaneously. As you read the words within this book, you are receiving the tools, lessons learned, and inspirational moments that helped me rise above the looming cloud of unworthiness to a life of realizing my purpose, worth, and greater calling.

This is what I hope you learn from this book: that you *can* be great.

God said in His Word that the whole creation is waiting for your manifestation.

For the creation waits with eager longing for the [manifestation] of the sons of God.

ROMANS 8:19 ESV/KJV MANIFESTATION

Isn't this amazing? This says clearly that you are not created to be a nonentity; you were not born to just move through life without impact. You are a pacesetter, and there is something in you that the world needs. Not just your community but the whole of creation is waiting for your emergence into greatness. You can trust and believe that.

Life Can Be Hard!

An indisputable fact we must all remember is that life presents us with hardships and unpredictable timelines. These disruptions from your every day tend to devalue your faith and confidence in humanity, nature, and God. There are times in life when everything looks confusing, and everywhere you turn appears to be a dead end. In life, there are times when the conditions you face become too difficult to live with and almost impossible to grapple with.

The world is facing a global pandemic called COVID-19 right now. While the pandemic hits all nations, nationalities, races, and cultures, humanity grapples for the right weapons, and the fight for wisdom to combat this virus continues to challenge the survival of the human race. The world gropes for answers on how to fight, reason with, and understand a phenomenon that is beyond description.

Every day, mainstream media releases new evidence of the devastating impact of COVID-19 (the invisible lining) across the world. News about scaling statistics of infected persons, as well as those who have died from the pandemic, have only compounded fear and despair among men and women. People are scared stiff as they struggle with how to remain safe during these uncharted times.

I hear the rhetorical questions many ask themselves: "Do I go to work despite the high possibility of contracting the virus, putting my family at risk? Or do I stay home and watch my family go short of food? Will this ever blow over; will life ever be normal again?"

While individuals face this dilemma, governments (states and nations) are at a crossroads in their attempt to find a balance. "How can we reopen without increasing the spread of the virus?" they ask. "Should we continue to stay and home while suffering a record decline in our economy?"

I am aware that presently, the occurrences around the world leave little room for hope. Many cities of the world that once teemed with a significant number of people now look like ghost towns. Everywhere you turn, you see people wearing masks, sheltering-in-place, with no visible end in sight. And through all of this, one thing seems to be startlingly clear: no matter how advanced humanity has become, she's ever helpless alone —without God.

These are the seasons where you even reach out to others for help, but it turns out to be an effort in futility. The people you think will be of help and whom you expect will stand by you just look the other way.

Many times, your focus shifts to self when this happens. You start looking inward, away from everyone else, including your Creator, the only One who can fix your problems. You begin to think you are alone, and you become so fixated on the unpleasant issues around your life that you simply forget and become very oblivious of He who walks with you.

You are unable to see the greatness in yourself because you allow your misguided thoughts to take you on an excursion far beyond your reality. This leaves you on the trail of bluebonnets and picket fences, which are not a part of your current reality or situation. And because you subconsciously or consciously say yes to such negative imaginations, you become stuck and completely unable to move beyond your reality, and before long, the feeling of hopelessness sets in. It is the repetitive negative thoughts that begin to cloud our current judgment. You may have heard the term "stinking thinking." This term is used to define how your perpetual negative thoughts give voice to your actions. Your actions now align to the self-fulfilling prophecy of depression, fear, and doubt to fame of few being realized in your life –the persuasive thought that you are not good enough and you cannot seem to accomplish a day-to-day task or your dreams. This is because you have allowed "stinking thinking" to influence **your greater**. This can set you on a trajectory of self-defeat, leading to a downward spiral of emotional breakdowns questioning your identity in Christ.

Amid uncertain times, you may question your faith. If you are not rooted in God, you may begin to wonder if God is still for you. Remember that God said in His Word,

I will never leave, never forsake you.

HEB 13:5; DEUT 31:6

Your spiritual stamina may start to shake; this is the point when most people seek alternatives to God. They see the world as being upside down and completely turned around, which is relevant today with the COVID-19 pandemic. But can I be honest with you? We have all been there a time or two—or three and even four. So you are not alone.

Moreover, do you desire to pick up your pieces and still go all out to win? Regardless of how tough and uncertain life has been, do you still want to make a mark on the sand of time? Do you see the possibility of the greatness in you emerging again? Are you anxious to pick up the torch and run through the dark tunnel of life till you see the light? Then you are holding the right book.

Right here begins the defining point of **your greater**. How you see yourself will determine your aptitude, therefore, causing a chain reaction of positive steps toward **your greater.** Author Craig D. Lounsbrough made a profound statement: "If you dare to dig deep enough, you will find a side of yourself that will dramatically enhance all of the sides of yourself." Meaning if you are willing to do the work, all of the negative perceptions and inhibitions you may feel will be forced to meet the greater person that resides within you.

You Can Sprout Again!

Rather than allowing what you are going through to draw you back, why not trust God to see you through? Hear what David said:

"

In my distress, I called upon the LORD; to my God,
I cried for help. From his temple, he heard my voice,
and my cry to him reached his ears.

PSALMS 18:6 ESV

You remember the story of Peter in Matthew 14:22-33. Jesus called Peter out of the boat, and he confidently walked on water toward Jesus. The walk was smooth, and he became a hero among other disciples. But suddenly, the wind became "boisterous." One translation of the Bible says the wind was "contrary." In other words, the normal condition of life can suddenly become contrary. A glimpse away from Jesus, and Peter began to sink. He was wise enough to call out to Jesus for safety.

Remember, this is your moment as you are redefining, reflecting, and taking inventory of where you are in life while answering a few rhetorical questions in your mind. How do I see myself? What are some of the challenges that are hindering my success?

Who are the people of influence in my life? As you ponder on these questions, remember the journey of a thousand miles begins with one single step forward. With each gradual step, momentum builds and cultivates a renewed identity and awareness of who you are becoming –**your greater**.

God Is for You!

Understand that God is not against you. He is ever for you, and he hasn't changed his mind concerning you. He desires to see you become great, and even right now, not later.

So, you need to change your perspective about yourself. Stop seeing yourself the way others see you or how your condition describes you. Start seeing yourself as God sees you.

Finally, we shall examine the place of vision and purpose in your quest for greatness. I will also share personal experiences with you to keep you encouraged. Just as I said earlier, you are not alone.

Also, at the end of each chapter, you will find ideas for personal commitment and lists of affirmations, which you can always use to stay energized and encouraged. The truth is that it all begins with you. As motivational speaker Brian Tracy says, "Your life only gets better when you get better"[2]. If you recall, Brian Tracy has authored over seventy books and written and produced over 300 audio and video learning programs, including the worldwide bestselling *Psychology of Achievement*. Brian is known for his invaluable lectures, speeches, and crowd-stirring motivational talks.

You can secure a new mental design, an inner construct that is rooted in God's Word that declares who you are. This is because nothing is the truth except the Word of God. Other things are mere facts. Whatever the Word of God calls you is not a suggestion but the truth. God is bound by His Word, and he cannot lie. So quit seeking approval from social media or friends.

Avoid being happy or sad based on a general view about you, but rather seek divine opinion. This is because all they can see is who you are today. But the Word of God speaks into your

[2] https://www.goodreads.com/quotes/629383

future. Your greatness has been spoken of already, and it is bound to come to pass. So get excited!

01

CHAPTER

Designed for Greatness: Discovering Your "Greater"

You were designed for accomplishment, engineered for success, and endowed with the seeds of greatness.

ZIG ZIGLAR

Whether you're a single mom or family man, you're in business, or you're working for someone, one thing is certain: you have your picture of greatness. It's somewhere on the walls of your mind, in the wallet, or your back pocket. Somewhere, somehow, you got a model for greatness, and you're always chasing after it.

If not, you've imagined yourself working in a particular field as a child or teenager. Just because right now, it doesn't look like the picture or image from the younger days does not mean you still cannot achieve your dreams, goals, or aspirations. What matters today is your starting point and the belief that you are worth it. Your past or current failures do not define you. The moment of change and transformation begins now!

But alas! This is the time to isolate and identify what greatness really means to you. It is time to walk in a new level of clarity about what makes it to the top of your priority list. By this, I mean, you get to where you courageously reset your priority.

You need to respond to the questions within your mind with an affirmative "yes." There's a voice that continually desires to ensure you're not wasting time or resources chasing something or someone who will dim your light of purpose. Remember, the journey begins and ends with you. The mental picture of yourself right now does not have to be well-defined or perfect. When I started writing this book, my flaws outshined the absolute truth of who I am in Christ. I was ashamed of what I had become because of my perfection, to be perfect at all times, and nothing bothered me, which was far from the truth. Just as I had to reflect on my model of greatness, you will have to do the same. Have you answered the question of priority?

Talking about priority, for many years, I thought the drive to my greater was rooted in how well I pleased others. I just desired to make people happy and to relieve someone's pains. And in the process, I enjoyed the response I got, the applause playing on the background of my mind. I was always glad because I felt needed. The fact that someone somewhere was calling on me filled my bucket.

If we are not careful, we can confuse the applause and the desired feelings of being needed as a means of honoring our gifts and talents. The reality is this has nothing to do with our purpose, passion, or destiny. However, the results of the masquerade can leave you hopeless, lonely, depressed, and insecure about who you are or who you are striving to become.

For me, the seeds were planted deep within; hopelessness grew and became the cause of my pain. For instance, I realized I was gradually losing touch with my family in my quest for greatness. I got it completely wrong. I can recall having a conversation with my son, who felt as though my attitude and behavior did not align with my actions at home. The relationship that I desired and attempted to cultivate was overshadowed by my lack of engagement, isolation, insecurities, and distained need to give everyone else 110% while giving my son less than 50%.

I was giving the world my best and breaking record performance at work. However, I was giving little at home because, by the time I got back home, I was already depleted from the day's work. I continued to succeed. Because of my ambition, not only did my son feel left out but the entire family. My son was determined to give voice to my destructive behavior. I want to pause right here to drop a nugget to all the fathers reading this book. Do not let your pride or ego get in the way of accepting criticism from your children or waving it off as if their position or feeling does not matter because of their age. Remain open-minded to hear and make the necessary adjustments as needed. We are responsible for the outcome of our children, and they should not be subject to our emotional trauma because the footprints we leave have a lifelong impact.

But later, I had to shift and change my thinking. I had to revisit my priority. At that moment, my desire shifted from applause to actual progress in my relationship with my son. I began to give my son the best of me.

And as soon as I shifted my priority, my son's attitude toward me shifted as well. I redefined what greatness meant to me. Do not give up because you do not see an immediate change in the dynamics of the situation or relationship. Remain diligent and consistent because you will see the fruits of your labor in the end.

Get ready to build positive mental images of yourself moving into your greatness as you read this chapter. You see, destiny is the outcome of interactions between divine and self-made designs. There's an essential relationship between our past, present, and future. I'm talking about a vine that has its roots in yesterday, its seeds in today, and its fruits in tomorrow.

Would you believe me if I said *we were all created to be beyond average? That our design was fashioned with the incredible in mind?* Consider the hands that lift glistening trophies, the heads that wear jeweled crowns, and the necks that are adorned with Olympic gold medals. Don't they look just like your design? Aren't you also sculpted for tremendous results and world-shaking achievements?

Let this thought soak in for a moment.

Now can we proceed? Maybe you've asked yourself the *big* questions: "Why am I here?" "What am I born to do?" "Am I even relevant to my world?" Well, the answers to your inquiry lie in your ability to understand and utilize your nature and design.

So until you come to a place where you understand the purpose of existence, you'll continue to struggle with reality. Imagine square pegs trying to fit in round holes. Talk about an epic fail! Likewise, many people are caught between the daily struggles, dealing with pain and regret without full awareness of how to navigate through the vast ocean of life.

This is because life consists of deliberately patterning your functions and activities according to divine stipulations and designs. By this, I mean discovering what you were made to contribute to humanity and investing every sweat that graces your brow to produce your foreordained greatness.

Thus, I believe that the art of living meaningfully is all about awareness and response to the present in the light of our understanding of who we are. Yet, many times individuals fail to recognize the opportunities in the present because their eyes are glued to the disappointments and failures of the past. And usually, when this occurs, you walk into seasons of depression and gloom, where thoughts run wild, and the negative pictures in our mind emerge untamed.

Do you have any idea what I'm talking about? Have you been here before? Have you tried to soar high in today's skies, and yesterday's mistakes said, "Stay low"? Did you decide to say yes to the future's beaming light of hope, and the past barked out, "Say no!"?

You're not alone! In truth, a person always has to wrestle free from mediocrity's clingy fingers before they can embrace greatness.

Origins of Low and No Mentalities

Evangelical author Charles R. Swindoll wrote, "Life is 10% what happens to you and 90% how you react to it."[3] And although this is true most of the time, you may find yourselves trapped in a crippled state of mind where unable to positively

---

[3] https://www.goodreads.com/quotes/1169-life-is-10-what-happensto-you-and-90-how

react to life's circumstances, unable to fully engage in the present.

How many times have you lost glorious treasures and future bounties by paying little or no attention to your mentality? Without being deliberate about what you think today? Indeed, every battle is first won or lost in your mind.

The most significant part of who you are or what you're becoming is less desirable because of the clanging cymbals of doubt and resounding bells of defeat that sound loudly within your minds. We often hear silent screams and voices that play, "Give it up!

It's not possible" in repeat mode.

People grapple with the familiar thought of "Should I stay or move!" And because of the clashing cymbals, they clam up, shut down, and decide within themselves that their potential and purpose are not worth fighting for. We all know the moments of wiping our faces for the last time before throwing in the towel.

Unfortunately, this will trigger a natural chain reaction and a perilous downward spiral when quitting. Because of this, the body and mind will align together, creating an accumulated jargon of thoughts and ideas that hinders one's ability to move forward. This cripple an individual, holding them hostage and unwilling to move out of their current comfort level.

Reflection

Right now, you have begun to absorb the context of defining your greatness or the greatness you desire to become. I want you to pause for a brief moment and complete this exercise. Grab a sheet of paper and fold the paper vertically. On the left side of the paper, list five areas that you want to change, on the right side, list the action word to achieve it. For example, if *pride* is an area I desire to change, my action word to achieve the desired change is *prayer*. This activity will begin to help you formulate the vision for change and redefining your greatness while taking actionable steps to achieve it. Taking these measurable steps will help you grasp a better understanding and working knowledge of your mental design and destiny as the tools necessary in defining your greatness.

Our Mental Design Is Our Destiny

Understand that no building can become bigger, better, or more beautiful than its architectural plan and design. Let's look at an example: Burj Khalifa in Dubai, which stands at 829.8m high as the tallest building in the world today, has 163 floors. Certainly, the citizens of Dubai didn't lazily crawl out of bed one sunny morning to find that massive edifice. No, they didn't. People painstakingly designed it. And it's not possible to have a design for a duplex and expect to construct a skyscraper.

What model do you have in your mind for your life? Building Burj Khalifa likely required the use of tools that would have been considered wasteful or undesirable for a duplex. What tools are you using for the plans in your life? Are you shooting for greatness or mediocrity?

I know you are wondering if I was ever in self-limiting circumstances as a leader, husband, father, or an associate pastor. As a leader, you live for every moment to count. I can recall leading this huge project at work. The project entailed instituting a new integrated technology platform throughout the school district. It involved many different moving parts such as teacher training, developing a professional learning community, ongoing professional development support for teachers, parents, and students. I know I made the people within my group and those around me miserable. The project had to be perfect, and my anal nature kicked it. My communication mannerisms or style became a language of "me" and not "we." I was selfish, not considerate of others' time, and very goal conscious. I placed so much pressure upon myself to get everything right (personal recognition and applause) that I lost myself in the process. My pride kicked in, and I imprisoned myself for years due to that experience and others similarly. I was lost in a world of me and could not see it. I had to begin redefining myself and who I was designed and created to be ... just as you are now looking to define or redefine **your greater**.

So yes, I've experienced the boundaries I placed on my own life; I've been my jailer. And from what I passed through, I learned that our fiercest battle comes from within, and the most vicious enemy is self.

At some point in my life, fear took center stage because I was adamantly unwilling (or maybe merely unable) to change the mental construct I had within. What did I get? Well, I was forced to look at the world around me from a narrow and limited scope or view. My mindset became so myopic that I couldn't see beyond what was around me. I was so overwhelmed with situations around me that they formed a major boundary around my mind, hindering me from thinking in line with greatness, which is "stinking thinking."

There were times that my thoughts overshadowed my spiritual understanding. My world looked as though it had turned upside down. I was feeling insecure, not good enough, broken, and depressed. And all I could do to stay calm at this point was to keep reassuring myself of who I am in Christ.

Believe me, the struggle was real, and the battle within was great. I never knew my thoughts could take so much control of me that I started to reflect the self-defeating thoughts by limiting my outward actions of God's love and purpose for my life. The Bible says that believers should give the devil no place. Yet that's exactly what I did.

Through prayer, praise, and reading God's Word, I was able to see God's purpose and plan for my life. I thought in my roaring thirties that I had it all figured it out and quickly realized that his plan is greater than I had ever imagined. You see, I left my thirties understanding that I had no real limitations and that the ability to do the unimaginable and achieve the impossible had been with me all the while. It was worked into my design; all I needed to do was see it and align accordingly. Yes, I can do all things through Christ who strengthens me. Remember: nothing is impossible; you must be willing to do the work. You are definitely worth the investment and do not allow self-destructive mental constructs to hinder your journey to **your greater**.

Holes in Our Mentality Equal Holes in Our Design

Due to your inability to grasp a reflection of eternal greatness in the one who created you, your perspective has become limited to the confines of your mind and the mental roadblocks set to distract you. These roadblocks leave you trapped and unwilling to move. They form a simulated reality and self-sabotaging imagery that create mental walls and hurdles on the free highways of life.

The truth is, self-sabotaging thoughts and self-limiting confessions are self-directed arrows. We can start with a complete mind X-ray! We can find the holes in our hearts: lacunas, vacancies, some emptiness that we wish were not there. This behavior impacts relationships, career goals, or limits your sight to see **your greater**. It is totally a frustrating or never-ending cycle that lowers your self-esteem and self-confidence. However, filling up those obvious spaces and boosting your self-esteem becomes difficult because you have now placed a self-limitation boundary within your design. Therefore, resulting in a defeated perspective of yourselves: you see inability instead of ability.

For example, living with self-doubt is like blowing air into a punctured balloon. Think about it. The air blown into the balloon is supposed to increase to make it bigger than its former self, but the holes drain all that awesomeness. Likewise, although you might have great potential, self-doubt saps all that greatness.

And surprisingly, these mental struggles are as ancient as time itself. The Bible tells of the fear of Israel before they entered into their promised inheritance. God had asked them to conquer a great city called Jericho, so their faithful leader—Moses—sent out from among them twelve spies to run surveillance on the territory.

As the story goes, ten of the spies returned with a negative, which I call "low" and "no" information. They told all the Israelites that the mission God had given them was an impossible one. According to them, the inhabitants of the land were undefeatable. They said the citizens of Jericho were giants, whereas—the poor Israelites—were as grasshoppers compared to them,

and we were like grasshoppers in our sight, and so we were in their sight.

NUMBERS 13:33 KJV

Did you notice that they were the ones who saw themselves as grasshoppers? Funny, isn't it? Alas, they failed to see the big picture. God had shown them their design. They were made to be fierce conquerors, but the gaping hole of low self-esteem and fear drained out all their victory.

You can reach beyond your will to find your strength to get back in the game. Try this activity to reengage or define your now. Identify a list of things that are preventing you from having what you desire. Give yourself a two to three-minute wait time as you evaluate your why, take the time to see what is holding you back. If you are afraid of failure, take time to list all the ways you succeeded in the past. Recount the ways by which you overcome fear. Let those emotions and behaviors drive your current reality to build momentum to **your greater**. Remember that failure, fear, and not feeling enough are okay to feel at some point in time in your life. You are not going to be perfect, and you will not always get it right or receive the desired outcome. Accept where you are and allow the place you are to guide you to **your greater** of new opportunities, new relationships, new career goals, a new perspective, and new friendships.

The Words We Speak, the Thoughts We Think

Usually, it is your mindset that starts with losing the battles of the mind through the mouth. Your mouth is the gateway to your realities; what you say and think about end up molding your realities in life, whether good or otherwise. It has been established that the power of intention, which is expressed basically through the thoughts in your minds and the words we speak, will eventually affect all things that matter to you. This goes to show that what you think and say will determine the trajectory of your life.

How you perceive yourself will generate positive or negative thoughts, determining success or failure. What you believe becomes your ultimate reality, causing your will and actions to respond in the same manner. If you lack self-confidence, you will approach life, beliefs, and goals from the glass half-empty instead of full. I can write the book on this one. Growing up, I lacked self-confidence because of my dark skin color as a young boy. At nine years old, I can recall asking my mother if she could buy me some bleaching creme because I thought if my skin were lighter, then my peers would stop teasing me. By my 6th-grade year in middle school, I had heard every black joke there was. It made me self-conscious, insecure, and I questioned everything about myself. Those insecurities manifested into adulthood because I could not see who I was in Christ and how much He loved me. So, you see, when you allow the enemy to win the battle of the mind, he's able to pull the strings as if you are a puppet in all directions.

No one finally arrives at a great height in life without first allowing the thought of greatness to dominate their mind. And this thought is seen even in their actions. Through this, you come to the awareness that you have unlimited abilities that are inherent in you, and that awareness motivates you to positively affect your life. That is, who you think you are and how you verbalize those thoughts is who you become. No wonder the Bible tells us,

Death and life are in the power of the tongue, and those who love it will eat its fruit.

PROVERBS 18:21 NKJV

So the question then is, what do we say when we're faced with hurdles on the track of greatness? What is your confession when you're challenged to higher standards?

You Need a Better Reflection

You have to come to a place where you become aware of the pictures that are painted in your mind because they'll eventually become templates for your future. What you see is what you become. This is a law in the realm of light and a universal principle that molds tomorrow.

Fortunately, you don't need to live under the shadows of someone else's achievement or greatness. Likewise, you don't have to be haunted by the negativity that has been spelled out against you by people you've trusted, loved, and respected. Everyone deserves a better and brighter reflection, which can only be found in God, our heavenly Father.

It's comforting to know that your true greatness is defined in the image of your heavenly Father. It is always unto you as far as you can see. So the question is, how high can you see yourself climbing the ladder of greatness?

Perhaps you still remember concave and convex mirrors as taught in elementary school. A sweet little girl picked up her momma's spoon and looked at it on both sides. One side showed that she was bigger but upside down while the outside of the spoon reflected a smaller but upright image. Well, one thought provoking thing about concave and convex mirrors is how they change what you see entirely. But how much of life is dictated by sight?

Now, it's not about what you set in front of the mirror; it's about the kind of imagery and reflections that you get from it. Concave and convex mirrors have different physical properties that alter the sort of reflection that they generate.

This means the side of the spoon that you choose will form your picture about yourself. Bigger or brighter, smaller or dimmer, erect or upside down; it doesn't matter who you are; it's simply about what you see on your side of reality.

Take a brief moment to pause and reflect on the following as you are conceptually defining your greatness; what reflection do you have about your life? Are you viewing your experience through a mirror that only diminishes your actual image of greatness? Do you see yourself less than who you are destined to be? It's high time you make a shift that changes your perception and perspective.

How Can We Turn This Around?

Sam Rayburn, the forty-third Speaker of the US House of Representatives, once said, "Readiness for opportunity makes for success. Opportunity often comes by accident; Readiness never does."[4]

---

4 https://archive.org/stream/journalofhouseof19nort_0/journalofhouseof19nort_0_djvu.txt

Do you agree with him? If you do, then I'd like you to ask yourself this question: Are you prepared for greatness? Yes, everybody wants success, but have you organized your mind and life into a state of readiness?

Most professional marathon runners will tell you that to achieve greatness, preparation is required. You cannot expect to hit the target or win the race without training. Preparation is the key to unlocking all the doors to achieve your greatness. Remember, you did not get here overnight, and it's going to take persistence and faith to move to **your greater** life.

Meb Keflezighi is an excellent role model, mentor, and one of America's greatest marathon runners of our time. He is the only athlete in history to win the Boston Marathon, the New York City Marathon, and an Olympic medal. His resilience and preparation began back in his home country of Africa before his family fled in 1987 to the US to escape a brutal war. Meb's determination to be a world-class runner was one of the driving forces that pushed him to greatness. Throughout his journey, he attributes preparation, persistence, and dedication as three characteristics that propelled him to stay in the race even when things around him looked unfavorable. No matter the test or obstacle, Meb's approach was to get up each day with a renewed mindset to give moment and opportunity his best. Allow Meb's story to help begin the building blocks to achieving **your greater**.

Moreover, just as Meb surrendered his will to achieve greatness, God is asking if you fully surrender and submit to Him. When you do, you will begin to see God embrace and surround you with His love like never before. There is the need to surrender to God because only the hand of God can fulfill the plan and purpose of God. God's plan for your life can only come to pass with His help. And He does not want strife with any man. Neither does He force His will upon anyone. Submission to His will gives Him full access to your life, and you are sure to arrive at His ordained greatness for your life.

Hence, it is critical to understand that will without faith is impossible. You can only fully surrender when your will and faith are joined as one. The will represents your mindset, determination, and grit to withstand, and faith ignites your hope and willpower to continue despite what it looks like. This is the winning combination to bring about change or a turnaround in your life.

Setting Versus Submitting to God's Grace

Hence, patience and desire for God are critical to your turnaround. Many have stopped themselves on the path to greatness and road to recovery because they set unrealistic goals. Some other people have failed because they neglected God's grace. Forgetting that without the grace of God, we cannot do or even become anything worthy on the earth.

The truth is that we all have some limitations that can hinder us from achieving greatness, but the grace of God is the catalyst that covers up our inadequacies and amplifies our efforts. Apostle Paul said,

❝

I am what I am by the grace of God.

1 CORINTHIANS 15:10, KJV

Even though he worked hard, he read continuously and prayed fervently, yet as he admitted, all that yielded result because of the seal of grace upon his life. I believe he knew that he needed grace now more than in the past.

The truth is, your turnaround will take some time. Nothing great happens suddenly. My neighbor would always say, "If you jump up, you will fall, but if you grow or climb up, you will stay up." One very necessary thing about growth is that it takes time. Whatever grows overnight will burn out before the end of the day. Everything that will give a lasting impact will always take time to process, nurture, or grow. Every purpose of God is time-bound.

Your destiny is beautiful, but there is always time for manifestation. But usually, the challenge is that you want it done quickly, you want to have it all at once, you want to arrive at the top quickly. Great men or women today didn't appear into greatness—they grew into it.

So I say to you, don't be hard on yourself. Your life and destiny are ever before God, and He will see to it that you achieve greatness, but at the right time. By this mindset, the power and strength that you will begin to gain while you wait will move you closer and closer to God.

More often than not, moving on to greatness requires the shedding of old baggage: friends, places, things, and acquaintances. Greatness demands that you release yourselves from strongholds of past experiences, negative thoughts, and fear.

Therefore, please do not be ashamed of your present reality. Instead, own it. Walk in the joy, knowing that you relinquished control and now ready to build new constructs of hope, faith, and love.

Say confidently and in a loud voice, "I give thanks to God because I am fearfully and wonderfully made; I am not an error or a specimen for an experiment. I am a masterpiece." The former you is dying, and the newness of **your greatness** is beginning to take root. Through these, you are planting new seeds that germinate with the watering of God's Word, a dedicated prayer life, daily affirmations, and realizing your new position and purpose in him.

Invest in Yourself

Richie Norton, an award-winning best-selling author of the book *The Power of Starting Something Stupid,* once said, "Every penny not spent on investing in yourself (after basic needs of course) may be a wasted future opportunity."[5] It takes personal responsibility to emerge outstanding in life. Your journey to greatness requires that you deliberately take actions toward investing in yourself and growth.

No matter the potential in a seed, when it is not nurtured, it will dry up from the root. Steady watering and pruning are necessary for the germination of a seed to fruiting. In the same way, you carry the seed of greatness in you. And this seed is of great worth. So take the time to be a better person every day. Learn something new, expose yourself to greater ideas. As much as possible, be better today than yesterday.

Here are five tips to help invest in yourself that will aid you to **your greater**.

1. Identify a specific time for prayer, meditation, and reading God's Word daily.
2. Create a vision board of your goals. Visualizing and seeing your goals daily will help you remain focus on the task ahead.

---

[5] https://www.eofire.com/podcast/richienorton2/

3. Create a daily or weekly check-in form to monitor your progress.
4. Journal your thoughts daily or weekly to keep yourself motivated and engaged toward the goals.
5. Celebrate small victories because they lead to you achieving your long-term goals.

Don't Be Discouraged. Keep Pressing

There will be times in life that you will have to encourage yourself when no one else will. Moments when it seems like you are on a lonely path, and no one even understands what you are going through.

Moments when the streams of tears run ceaselessly down your face. Moments when the only option is to turn back to your comfort zone.

Everyone who has achieved greatness can testify to the fact they were discouraged at one time or the other. The path to greatness once looked like a closed road to them. And believe me, this is the defining moment for everyone. It's the point where a lot of people with great dreams are sieved out, and they settle for mediocrity because they lack that inner strength to keep pressing.

A typical example from the Bible about a man named Job comes to mind. We learn that Job had a consistent walk with God while everything in his life was normal and enjoyable. There was a man in the land of Uz, whose name was Job; and that man was perfect and upright, and one that feared God, and stayed away from evil. ... His substance also was seven thousand sheep and three thousand camels, and five hundred yokes of oxen, and five hundred she asses, and a very great household; so that this man was the greatest of all the men of the east. (Job 1:1, 3 KJV)

This man had an unbroken dedication to God. He was blessed until he became great. His greatness was noticed in all the regions of the east which was the seat of civilization in those days. You might think it easy to serve God and follow him while things are cozy and smooth. Yes, but that wasn't Job's style.

At some point in his life, Job was challenged. He lost all his children, his business collapsed, and he became bankrupt—all in one day. I tell you, this would break anyone, especially considering Job couldn't point at one fault of his own as the cause. Not because he did anything wrong, or he went into a wrong business deal. At that point, even his wife was ashamed of him and advised him to curse God. His friends came around and worded him up! I can imagine them saying, "This pain and agony is too much, Job. Give up on your commitment to God, seek alternatives, and bend your rules a little bit."

Rather than giving in to their advice, see what Job did.

Job stood up and tore his robe in grief. Then he shaved his head and fell to the ground to worship. He said,

"

I came naked from my mother's womb, and I will be naked when I leave. The LORD gave me what I had, and the LORD has taken it away. Praise the name of the LORD!"

JOB 1:20-22 NLT

In all of this, Job did not sin by blaming God. Can you ever imagine that? A man in his condition!

We learn that Job had a consistent walk with God, even when *everything* fell apart. Friends, in your relationship with God, always remember that He is sovereign—He sees the beginning and the end; so you must respond to His sovereignty with worship to him instead of doubt, bitterness, or anger. Truth is God is never averse to you, No! He is always on your side at all times.

However, Job was determined to wait. He said,

❝

But I will wait for better times, wait till this time of trouble is ended.

JOB 1:20-22 NLT

Waiting is a sign of perseverance. And understand that it is not the time we spend waiting that matters but our attitude while we wait. Job was hopeful, and he knew this time would end. He was confident he was destined for greatness, and no matter what was happening, his greatness was assured.

The good news was that in the end, God restored his greatness. In fact,

❝

The LORD gave Job twice as much as he had before.

JOB 42:10

This was possible because he pressed on in faith and commitment to God. His flame of hope didn't stop burning.

The same goes for you: during your trying moments, do not let your mental construct take over your life. Instead, let the situation draw you closer to God. Make it a habit to always draw strength from God. He is always there to help you through when your energy cannot take you anymore. When it looks like all hope is lost, simply raise your head to the hills where divine help comes from.

King David said in Psalms 42:5,

Why art thou cast down, O my soul? And why art thou disquieted in me? Hope thou in God.

KJV

So rather than being cast down, hope in God. Instead of entertaining any pity party around your life, stay encouraged, and keep moving. The tunnel may look dark, but there is light at the end.

When looking up to God becomes your usual response to issues, you will always receive energy to keep pressing. The great scientist Albert Einstein once said. "Life is like riding a bicycle. To keep your balance, you must keep moving."[6] Therefore, stay the course because you are on a journey to **your greater**. And it's a marathon, not a sprint.

Hold on to Greater Confessions

It is time to renew our commitment and willingness to unveil what we have sown into the fabric of our minds. We have to open our mouths to speak life into the situations we hacked and axed down with our tongues.

Remember when you said, "I don't think I'll finish this project," or "This Ivy League school is not for people of my race, color, financial, or social background"? Remember when you said, "I can't have that job, promotion, profit, house, home, family, and love life"? It's time to unwind all these things in your mind. You need a release! You need a comeback!

By this, I mean you look straight into a reflection of yourself and speak greatness into your life. I mean you begin to boldly confess, "I am willing to grab hold of my future by realizing who I am and who I am created to be."

---

[6] https://quoteinvestigator.com/2015/06/28/bicycle/

Personal Commitment

Today, make a personal commitment to define or redefine my greatness. Release your mind from every limitation, and begin to see yourself in the eternal image of your heavenly Father. No more mediocre thought and words. Resolve to see, think, and speak greatness from now on.

Affirmations

- No matter how I feel about my current reality, I unwind all negativity that is woven into the fabric of my mind.
- I believe I can achieve greatness.
- I love, value, and appreciate myself for who I am and who I am becoming.
- Everything happening right now is for my ultimate good. Therefore, I am willing to grab ahold of my future by realizing who I am and who I am designed to be.

02

CHAPTER

Taking Off the Mask: Identifying Barriers to Greatness

And when the curtains fall,
We trundle back to the shadows—
Relieving ourselves of the masks that
shield us from the world

DIWA

The beauty in life is better appreciated in the glory of the light. You must have heard—countless times—of people who love watching the sunset or the sunrise. They are swept off their feet when the sun's rays fall upon a lush green hill in all its fiery glory, painting the lilies and daffodils in brighter shades. Yes, people love it when the flight takes off and they can close the curtain and remain hidden. The mask represents the face the world sees; however, underneath the mask, the person's identity presents hidden secrets, insecurities, fears, and challenges that hinder you from achieving **your greater**. I know this too well. I lived in a world of wearing multiple masks. I thought as long as I kept up the appearances, no one would see my pain, hurt, or wounds. Most confusingly, the mask felt empowering to a degree because I was able to escape my current reality. I felt more comfortable wearing the mask and exchanging the mask to fit any situation.

If you are like me or simply experiencing this, the hurt, pain, and wounds will manifest in your career, relationships, goal attainment, and much more if not unmasked. As you embrace this chapter, leave yourself vulnerable to see yourself authentically. What I mean by authentically is simply transparent (be real with you). Be willing to fully unmask so that you begin to define or redefine **your greater**. You are becoming a healthier you more vibrant version of God created you is solely based upon your willingness to be truthful and honest with yourself. There is no fear in the One who created you. Realize the continuation of the journey rest in your ability to dig deep and extract all that you are becoming and redefining who you are in your greatness.

In contrast, most people get anxious and threatened when their mask is taken from them. This is because, other than being negative, sometimes a mask can offer a degree of protection. Likewise, the mask may promise to temporarily shield us from pain, shame, and sorrow, but it won't support our survival, growth, and manifestation.

Usually, we think we're doing a great job with the masks we're placing over our reality. But all this hiding does is give us a false sense of being. And in truth, our experience in various areas of life will be more worthwhile and meaningful if we live without false identities and misplaced hope of the past. How you approach, the world is based upon how you see yourself. If you are under the reality of colored lenses that align with your current reality, then you are living untruth to reach your full potential. Because you present something different underneath the mask and what you'll find is those hidden realities will surface and impact every area of your life.

Susan Sparks writes in *Psychology Today* (2015) that people hide behind masks for many different emotional responses. If you are insecure, the most common way it will manifest is through the mask of name dropping. If you are unsure of your power, then you hide behind the mask of being a bully. And finally, if you associate the world, who does not love you, then you mask it with anger. These hidden masks shape the direction of your life and present mistruths which causes an altered reality and keeps you from achieving **your greater**[7].

However, the truth is, you may have a mask on even when you don't intend to. It's like a protective gear or a defense mechanism. So what's your own story? What's your truth? Where's your reality? Is it beyond or beneath the mask?

Interestingly, social psychologists define masking as a process in which humans change or "mask" their natural personality to conform to social norms or conventional expected behaviors.[8] This means wearing a physical mask (which of course is not what I'm presenting) is a one-time action, while the true kind of spiritual, mental, and emotional masking is a *process* that has a wider scope of consequences.

The truth is, your mask can be your best friend and your worst enemy, all at the same time. You need to get to a place in your life where you discover the freedom of living in your truth and thriving despite your reality.

But who said this would be easy?

Sometimes it's more challenging to come to terms with yourself when you feel the weight of gravity on your shoulders, so you feel pressured to give up and give in to the pain and

---

[7] https://www.psychologytoday.com/us/blog/laugh-your-way-wellbeing/201510/the-masks-we-wear

[8] https://www.ifioque.com/social-psychology/masking

challenges in your life. The weight of the mask is unbearable, yet you tend to look the other way instead of facing the truth. What's the truth?

How can you explain your experience with the loss of focus in life and lack of strength to peel the first layer of the mask? You've been so accustomed to wearing the changing faces. But more often than not, you get by without realizing how these masks have crippled and invaded every thought and action—living day-to-day, under the perspective of feeling not enough—hoping that someone will eventually look beyond the mask to see and rescue you. But from who? From you?

Reflection

Now, I'm not talking about finding the next best outer appearance, but a discovery of who you really are on the inside. How long have you lived so scared and fearful of removing the next layer of the mask, so that people can see who you truly are? How much longer do you want to remain masked?

***

Three Layers of Masks

You see, more often than not, the heart and mind are usually trapped beneath the layers of three identified masks, and we are unable to move forward to our **greater**. Our **greater** is lost and hindered because of unwillingness to unmask these three elements. And for us to break free and break ahead to our next level of greatness, we must address these areas in our lives. But how do we do this? And just as Nicodemus asked Jesus if he had to go back into his mother's womb, we might ask if we need to go back in time. Not at all! The solution is not time travel. The goal is to identify where you on the path to self-discovery realizing that each path is different. It is not about how fast you progress but the steps to achieve success in your life. Look at like this: A sprinter takes off with more momentum and speed and, if not careful, will exert all of their energy and without force and energy to finish the race strong. However, a sprinter who understands that it takes more than momentum and speed to win a race will pace and adjust along the way to reach his or her final destination. Listen, breathe, and mediate as you dig into the three layers of masks.

The answer to your sprint is a thorough soul search. Yes, it is through deep and critical reflection that you can determine how one or all three of these elements impact or impede your daily life. The real work begins as you begin to unpack these varying masks in your life. And although this exercise might be painful and a little unnerving, it is the sure way to your desired outcome. Before we move too far into this concept of masking, I'll like to let you in on three layers of the masks that we all wear: The *Pleasing Mask*, the *Mask of Brokenness*, and the *Unforgiveness Mask*.

These three layers are interconnected. However, their manifestations may not appear at the same time, and each may impact your life exclusive of the others. These masks are conscious or subconscious blockers that will hinder you from fully walking into **your greater**. They connect or align together as an emotional sphere of influence that shapes your attitude, behavior, and belief about yourselves. Many times, you will find yourself lost in a mask unable to see yourself or what you've become. The Pleasing Mask identifies as the mask who wants to make everyone comfortable. The Mask of Brokenness identifies itself in the emotional stratosphere of anger, resentment, hurt, or pain. Lastly, the Unforgiveness Mask presents itself as a coping mechanism of bitterness and unresolved manifestations that contradicts a person's thoughts, mood, and perceptions toward others.

Consider a child whose father said, "Boy, I regret having you as a son!" or "Because of you, I curse the day I met your mother." Wow! Such powerful but negative words. Imagine the pain of rejection and the poisoned arrows of a toxic tongue shot straight from the bows and bowels of the man you call "Daddy." Now, parents should never say such a thing to their kids because most times, such harsh words do irreparable damage. And in this case, that boy may live the rest of his life in the chasm of that statement and under the three-layered mask of a wrong mentality.

When this boy needs validation and affirmation, he may become addicted to doing too much to please everyone, including the man who brought him down. Ordinarily, there's nothing wrong with pleasing people or doing what others admire, but the boy in question might want to do certain things just to avoid sinking in the narrow well of broken esteem.

And even as he grows to become an adult, everything he does might be tailored or fashioned to please others, probably because he doesn't want further rejection and disappointment. As a result, he would end up unhappy and frustrated because even if he achieves success, it wasn't for himself but for others.

Hence, we can say that such a person is wearing a broken mask. By this time, you can expect that the problem will surely progress because it's a catch-22, an unending chase. This boy who heard such vile words from his father will neither eventually please everyone nor find healing for his brokenness. All he can expect are manifestations of a festering condition of unforgiveness and bitterness that remain as a layer mask and malignancy.

The Pleasing Mask

Have you ever come across an animal more eager to please than a dog? Think about it! You can ignore your pet all day and neglect feeding it until you get back from work, yet when it sees you, it'll be eager to play with you and please you. Why do dogs do this? It's their nature. They are such needy creatures. No wonder the saying goes, "As loyal as a dog."

On the other hand, human beings are not pets, and what's cute in a dog is disgusting in a person. But sadly, many people are helpless people-pleasers, like clingy puppies. This is because they're wearing a pleasing mask.

A pleasing mask is the covering and layer that we place on our lives because something is injured on the inside. People with a pleasing mask have had experiences that make them emotionally dependent on others. They don't have a healthy sense of identity. Instead, they derive their personality and confidence from the opinions of others. And as a result, they tend to go to extremes to please others for validation and acceptance.

Moreover, I believe that you will have varying degrees of this mask operating in their lives. And although you might not be obsessed about pleasing everyone, you are often helpless to resist. Alas, the urge to please others often clouds our perception of responsibility, self-judgment, and thoughts about life. You think from a position of pleasing others first before we look to pleasing ourselves.

Let's look at Adam and Eve, who decided to seek cover behind leaves after the fall to help you understand further. God had commanded that Adam and Eve not eat from the forbidden tree. If they ate from the tree, they would surely die. The word die is symbolic of spiritual death, not physical death. However, they ate from the tree, and their eyes were open to the nature of sin, realizing they knew no sin before eating from the tree. They tried to mask their sin and shame with stuff that couldn't do the trick. Fortunately, God is Light. And so he called Adam and Eve to a place of truth and accountability. Could it be that masking became our second nature and a generic persona to the fallen man?

For instance, God spoke specifically to Adam and about the tree in the Garden:

Do not eat from this tree.

GENESIS 2:17, KJV

However, when Eve approached Adam with many reasons to eat, he indulged, therefore, what God had already spoken. Yes, Adam wasn't deceived like Eve; he sinned willfully.

Adam may have indulged because he was persuaded by Eve's rationale, rather than wanting to please Eve. Biblical scholars write books about these interpretations. Many times, we are so interested and concerned with pleasing others that we forget the One who we should be ultimately pleasing, which is our heavenly Father.

You see, when we please God, everything falls in line according to his will and divine purpose. The **greater** can have a fluid flow, thereby pushing us into our divine destiny. Moreover, we must understand that God is not pleased with masks and shifting shadows. He doesn't want his children to wear disguises but to be healed and shine as a light in the world.

The reality of working too hard to please people is the transposed truth and off-beam belief that someone will eventually like and admire us. That we'll earn love and respect. Somehow, we're more concerned about what people will think than about our happiness. You expect people to think highly of you because you put them first. There's something wrong about this picture!

Now, many will think this is okay. They'll wonder why I'm addressing it from this perspective. Well, I'm not against sacrifices and love, but the key, which is balance, must not be lost. I mean the kind of balance that does not leave you empty and nonresponsive.

Many times, the pleasing spirit leaves you the individual broken, disappointed, worn out, and lacking due to constant giving and giving without pouring back into yourself. This is true because I know many of you have had similar experiences in your marriages, jobs, childrearing, church activities, and church leadership.

You felt it was expected that you give in this degree with little to no support. You think it is found in receiving the accolades of success, however, pleading with yourself on the inside. Yes, pleasing is rewarding and gratifying for a while; but when reality set in, it became an additional responsibility or a heavy burden. The pleasing mask surfaced, and the unreal smile gripped both corners of your mouth. So you continued to smile while suffering secretly throughout yourself.

Are you tired yet?

I know the pleasing mask feels hopeless, and a level of despair fills your current reality, a reality where the one whom you see every day is being lied to by the false realities within your conscious state of mind. It reminds you every day of your past experiences, disappointments, failures, fears, and shortcomings.

Too often, you find yourself wearing a pleasing mask.

My Experience

Just a few years ago, I found myself unwilling to move due to the weight and gravity of life; it was a low time in my life. Inwardly, I struggled with an endless valley of emptiness, but to others, I seemed successful, hopeful, and full of life. My life didn't look shabby in any way. I was a high-level administrator in K-12 public education. I had a great family with an amazing wife and three children. And as a faculty member in higher education and associate pastor serving in the local church, life was almost perfect!

Life was moving at a rapid speed and I could not escape the feelings of loneness and despair. All of my life I needed to please everyone. As I recall some of my childhood memories, I was big on pleasing my friends and everyone around me to prove to myself that I was good enough. For me, their acceptance was far more valuable than anything which followed into adulthood. I equated acceptance with people around me being happy even if I had to forsake myself in the process. I had the "cannot say no" syndrome; I couldn't say no to anyone. I would work myself to depletion only to receive minimal in return. As a result of the pleasing mask, I fell into a deep level of anger, resentment, and frustration of which impacted my relationships and professional commitments. The grip of the pleasing mask has consequences that will not allow you access to **your greater** from within. This is due to your inability to dig into your inner consciousness because it is overcrowded with negative emotions that impact **your greater**, right now.

But one thing I remember telling myself was this: "Boy, you deserve to be comfortable as well." Remember, I stated earlier that you wear a pleasing mask to make everyone around you feel comfortable because you are secretly uncomfortable with who you are.

Reflection

As you reflect on this set of questions, I want you to close your eyes while doing some deep breathing exercises to try to find your inner strength to release every false belief about yourself. Can you relate to this? What part of yourself are you hiding or masking with false disguises? Who can hear the silent screams on the inside, saying, "This cannot be it." Yes! I have been there. And I am perfectly acquainted with the silent torment.

***

In the same way, my pleasing nature complicated life for me and wrapped me up in a whirlwind of mental exhaustion till I nearly burned out; I was trying to please everyone while screaming NO on the inside, yet no was the exact word I was unwilling to utter. I unwisely thought that I had to give everyone an extra 110%—and I was getting nothing, and getting little to no rest trying to complete every project with a better than perfect outcome. And the crazy part is that so many things fell through the cracks while I was busy trying to please everyone.

What I didn't understand was that the handclaps and cheers of success were my driving force. But I was focusing on the wrong thing and was misusing the exact thing that would have helped me discover my true design and end the charade that my life had become.

Eventually, it became obvious that I needed to get myself out of that abyss of frustration and self-torture from the pleasing mask. Remembering the Scripture,

Faith without work is dead.

JAMES 2:26, KJV

I knew that the converse was true too. I need both faith and work in my life to offer some stability. I quickly had to readdress my thoughts and actions.

Alternatively, I was overcome with emotions. I couldn't believe that I, by my omission, someone who was considered to be a control freak, was out of control mentally and spiritually in a drought. Not only was I giving to everyone else and neglecting myself, but I had left off filling myself afresh with the One who created me in His image. At least if I had just worked on my relationship with God during such hard times, I would have been comforted.

Yet my mental and spiritual life were not the only areas of my existence in danger. Indeed, it is a stark reality to know that not only is your spiritual relationship suffering, but your family also. I had to begin to replace works with balance and a pleasing spirit with faith.

The Broken Mask

Have you been broken and bruised due to past hurts, failures, and traumatic experiences? How can a doctor fix you when you hide your pain? How can a mechanic fix your car if you cover it in your garage? How can the wound within you heal when you act like it isn't there? Sometimes we feel crushed under the mill of life. We lose the sweetness and pleasantness of everyday experiences and look toward masking our painful reality. This may be a reason why many people continue to live life from not only a pleasing mask but from a broken mask too.

Unfortunately, the broken mask seeks to define your today and twist your hopes for a greater tomorrow. It leaves you in deep condemnation and judgment of yourself—a false reality of truth that you are not worth the greater! And you were never made for better!

Consequently, your mind and heart will only pump lies, fears, and weaknesses, and the enemy may dangle memories and experiences from your past to paralyze your present and alter the future. But you don't have to hide any longer. There's a way out, and the first step is coming clean with yourself. Ask yourself this honest question: Am I tired of my situation?

The Lady with an Issue She Could Hide

As I talk about being tired of your situation and desperate for a change, I am reminded of a woman found in Luke 8:43-48. She's a typical example of someone completely fed up with her broken mask.

This woman who had an issue of blood—a bleeding condition—realized **her greater** from a broken mask, and realized that she could not help herself. She looked to others for support. She endured trial and error from doctors who unintentionally cashed in on her predicament. Everything she had was gone except her hope, her final hope for a greater life. All the while, she received physical healing to cure that which only a spiritual awakening could heal.

She had been cast out and isolated because of her illness and eventually decided to reach out to God for help. She began to self-examine, realizing that she had done all that she could do. So in her broken state of mind and existence, she decided to regain her renewed passion and hope again because of her healing. She decided to move to **her greater**.

Thus, when this woman heard that Jesus was traveling through her neighborhood, she realized that help was near. Just as she was beginning to resign to her condition, she began to hear news of a prophet who healed people by having physical contact with them.

Her mask of brokenness permitted her to accept her condition for twelve long years. Throughout those years, she attempted to fight; however, she was unsuccessful. I know many of you can identify with the woman of trying and trying and never receiving a break. Imagine the disappointment after disappointment she must have felt for twelve long years. This woman, who suffered for these twelve long years, heard that Jesus was going to pass through her city, so she decided to take a leap of faith and touch the hem of Jesus's garment as He was walking through a crowded multitude of people. This story, which is found in the book of Luke 8: 40-48, declares that when she touched the hem of his garment, she was immediately healed.

This was incredible! Exactly what she needed! The testimonies were awesome; many miracles had been performed; the promise was attractive but not without a cost: she would have to unmask by denying herself and reaching for a better promise found in Christ to reach **her greater**.

Fortunately, her inner desire to be made whole from her brokenness was stronger than the comfort of remaining unexposed. So eventually, she got on a quest to seize the moment of her victory by her willingness to reach out for help through Christ.

In truth, before you can see any positive and permanent changes in your life, you have to be willing to seize the moment, moving beyond your current reality of despair to see who you are in Christ. The woman who had an issue of blood took advantage of the moment and made her way to Jesus amid a mammoth crowd. She was coming from a place of humility, struggling on her knees, pushing her way through, unwilling to return behind the veil that held her for so long.

And just like this courageous woman in the Bible, you have to initiate your recovery; you need to begin the healing process. Therefore, you must be willing to push through those emotions of doubt, rejection, and fear. This woman didn't let anyone or anything stop her. She pushed through to Jesus at an arm's length, and she extended her hands to touch the hem of his garment.

Instantly, she was rewarded! She received total and complete healing on a spiritual, mental, and, more evidently, a physical level. Finally, the longstanding and ceaseless menstrual flow stopped. And all this happened because she took the first step toward securing her greatness by being unafraid to reach out to God for help.

Now, here's an essential question that Jesus asked amid the thronging crowd. He said, "Who touched me?" And this poor, humble woman—terrified and in awe of what had happened to her—revealed herself to Jesus as the culprit. She was frightened because she didn't know what could happen next.

Interestingly, when Jesus saw this woman, he said, "Woman, your faith has made you whole." Beyond just getting healed, she found wholeness!

Reflection

Consider this desperate lady's story. Is she any different from you? Isn't there something from your past or in your present that has crushed and marred you? Well, here in this story lies your answer. So, are you willing to move and position yourself even in your broken state? Strengthen hope and revive faith! Be prepared to deny "self" and forsake pride to receive your full mental and spiritual healing and wholeness. Also, note that the woman with the hemorrhage surrendered her masks. Likewise, we must be willing to surrender the masks on our mind, body, and spirit to receive the fullness of God.

Hiding Your Brokenness behind the Façade

The woman who had an issue of blood was getting choked up under her mask. Her hiding places and broken masks began to fall apart under the burden of deterioration. She had to unmask. And, I believe, so do you!

Ariana Dansu, author of the famous poem "She Made Broken Look Beautiful, and Strong Look Invincible"[9], wrote a poem that accurately describes what it means to mask brokenness. The truth is, brokenness *can* be masked, hurt *can* be hidden away, and pain *can* be ignored. But what does it mean

---

[9] https://tyrannyofpink.com/2017/02/20/

to make brokenness look beautiful and walk the universe with your shoulders lifted like it's a pair of wings?

Reflection

Surely the pain and shame of brokenness always compel you to settle for a protective layer or covering.

But do you know what it means to live behind the shadows of your pain and run as fast as you can away from reflections of your shame? If yes, then you can relate to what I'm saying.

Sometimes, it means numbing the pain with drugs, drowning the whispers in the noise, and mopping the tears with smiles on an elastic face. Where's the veil? What's your mask? Is it the activity without identity, motion without progress, or feigned success, accolade, and sophistication without substance, satisfaction, and rest? 📖

The Unforgiveness Mask

A description of Sherrie McCorkle's book *Hidden Unforgiveness* reads, "The unforgiveness hidden in our memories is like an iceberg—90 percent is buried beneath the surface in our minds."[10] What a powerful statement! Sometimes unforgiveness exists that we are no longer aware of.

This past year, I had a good friend who wanted to take his life due to unforgiveness in his life. His unwillingness to forgive himself for his past impeded his future. Wes grew up together in a small city outside of Oklahoma City, Oklahoma. He came from a middle-class family; however, he decided to take a different set of directions around age twenty-one. Due to life circumstances, he decided to start selling drugs to make money, which eventually led him to serve approximately six years in prison. He never got the opportunity to fulfill his high school dreams of completing college and never achieving the American dream of success. Every time we talked, he frequently spoke negatively about himself. During one of our conversations, he stated "I am a loser and a convict, and my past wrongdoings will not allow me to be successful. I choose to take my life and end this suffering because I will never be able to be anything more than what I am today, which is nothing." Luckily, I was able to speak with him consistently that day, and through continuous prayer and declaring God's Word over his life, he decided not to go through with his plan.

You see, unforgiveness can become an inner illness and internal anomaly that you tend to always hide away. You need to

---

[10] https://www.barnesandnoble.com/w/hidden-unforgiveness-sherriemccorkle/1129426983

talk about this in a world where everything and everyone seems to be falling out and falling apart due to unresolved issues.

Usually, like smoke under a trash can, unforgiveness will be exposed, discovered, and revealed. But how many times have you sat over a well-sealed smokebox, thinking that no one will see the bitterness, darkness, and hurt you try to contain? That no one will hear the audible sighs of pain?

Voices in your head won't stop yelling, "Be nice to him, just avoid him or her, don't talk to them, why should you let it out, the wound will heal, don't even shed a tear, act smooth and cool, and then, everything will be all right." But will it?

The truth is, unforgiveness is a seed, and it will surely grow and bear sour fruits of regrets and pain. Unforgiveness is a poison to the mind and cancer to the soul. It must be exposed, unmasked, and released.

And like a tumor, it calls for a swift surgical response before it begins to shut down the vital organs of your life.

Unfortunately, unforgiveness has a bittersweet taste. There's a false sense of power and control— especially over people, issues, and circumstances— when harboring unforgiveness against people in your life So instead of enduring the sense of weakness, humility, and vulnerability of forgiveness, you choose to hold it back and mask it up. Imagine holding an uncapped grenade to your chest!

Also, it's a paradox to find that you sometimes hold yourselves behind the bars of unforgiveness. Your unwillingness to forgive yourselves for past and present hurts always haunts and hurts you. You do not realize that your willingness to forgive is not only for others but for yourselves as you begin the healing process.

Unforgiveness leaves you depressed and angry, caged and cornered, unable to make relevant progress, even in your relationship with God. You become tortured by imageries of victimizations and unrealistic realities.

Realize that there are many ways unforgiveness may manifest itself demonstrating expressions of hidden unforgiveness and bitterness. The mask will always give away some salient and subtle attitudes, actions, and reactions that testify to the hidden hurts, pain, and unforgiveness. You can equate the unforgiveness mask to this example: if you "told a lie" to your best friend and felt guilty about lying, you wouldn't be forgiven, nor justified in asking God to forgive you, and think that telling a lie in the first place wasn't wrong.

It's easy to entertain self-sabotaging thoughts as they relate to harboring unforgiveness. From the shelf of the mind, you pull down emblems of hope and crafts of greatness. Thoughts of greatness are hard to formulate while you're being consumed with pervasive, negative, unforgiving thoughts. You can't capture and retain feelings of personal success and greatness as you try to forget the times you've never agreed to forget—the times you've messed up, failed, fell, embarrassed, and hurt yourself. Gradually, you percolate the thoughts of self-defeat and failure. You can't see a bigger picture, and you seriously doubt a better future.

How can you win in life when you're constantly beaten down on the inside?

On the other hand, the mask of unforgiveness can make you easily irritable, angered, and provoked by the same person we think you have forgiven and the same issue you think is already bygone. You tend to replay the scenes of the offense, unconsciously strengthening the cords of unforgiveness.

It's time to unmask and face the reality of your inner pain. You have embraced the lies, promises, and threats that keep you hidden away behind the veil. It is time to release people and issues in your life. It's time to let out the snake from the basket. It's time to walk in freedom and true power. When you forgive, you unveil, you step out of the darkness and into the light, and you become unmasked and unchained.

Personal Commitment

Today, make a personal commitment to consciously and deliberately take off whichever mask you have on right now that has veiled you from the beauty and reality of life. Rather than hiding behind the mask to please others and remain hurt, unmask yourself, and embrace the wholeness in Jesus. Try this simple exercise. Think about a negative message you have received. Was the negative message truth? More than likely, the message was not true. You might want to ask yourself, why am I carrying around this message? What would happen if I decided to put it down? More than likely, nothing would happen. The point of the matter is the risk of allowing yourself to face a different reaction. The reaction is not to destroy but to help unveil the real up. Do not feel ashamed or threaten to allow people to see the real you. Allow the Word of God to be your reality. Let go of past hurt, and embrace the forgiveness in the finished work of Christ.

Affirmations

- I know I have lived behind the veil of so many realities of life.
- I have severally carried more than I can bear, but now I take off the veil.
- I allow the light of truth to shine into my life.
- I am not seeking to please people at my expense anymore, even though I will make sacrifices.
- I unmask myself and move in the direction of my healing and wholeness.
- I am not staying one more day nursing any hurt and pain.
- I deserve to be happy, so I take steps to secure my happiness.
- I choose to forgive myself, so I can forgive others around me.

Today I *unmask*

03

CHAPTER

Adjust Your Lens: Embracing the Savior Self

And You see what you choose to see
because all perception is a choice ...

PAUL FERRINI

Remember, attaining **your greater** is a process that requires digging to unpack so you can live out your true purpose as you walk, speak, and enjoy greatness.

Are you ready to board the plane of truth while cruising at an altitude 30,000 ft.? To reflect, journal, and discover the real you as your heavenly Father sees you?

Now fasten your seatbelt, you're on the airline of truth, and your plane is preparing for takeoff. This might be the last and final call before you get in the air. You may experience some turbulence before you hit your cruising altitude of 30,000 feet, but do not fear or retreat, nor get fixated on the situation. Rest assured in the One who created you. God is here to fly alongside you to protect you and ensure your safety.

However, your obedience to the process will determine your outcome and success. You need to cooperate with the pilot. He's your loving Father. So hold on tight so you can see and experience the warmth in the embrace of your loving Father, who simply adores and loves you.

To achieve **your greater** requires adjusting your lens to fit the depth and breadth of your journey. By doing this, you will increase your productivity, courage, and mindset. You can change jobs, relationships, and **your greater** results by seeing yourself in a new way. When God created "you," he formed, shaped, and purposed your destiny. Consider how no physical or mental feature was left out. Your design is perfect, and you have to believe that. Do not fear to hold onto this rightful knowledge while taking an insightful ride into realizing the truth.

Sometimes, some people struggle to see the change they can have based upon the false notion of not wanting to adjust their lens. Rather than giving direction to their greatness, they become victims of procrastination. Greatness resides within everyone; however, you must take every opportunity to make it happen.

And concerning this, Marcus Aurelius, a Roman emperor and a stoic philosopher said, "Everything we hear is an opinion, not a fact. Everything we see is a perspective, not the truth."[11]

How much effort you are willing to put into finding your true reflection?

Beyond the physical eyes, we all have the inner eyes that serve to produce our insight.

Adjusting your lens has nothing to do with altering your reality, but it has everything to do with *changing* your perception of your reality. It has to do with viewing your reality through different eyes. As with your physical vision, you may need to use a pair of recommended or fashionable glasses to change *how* you see *what* you see, not to change what you see.

I believe the most crucial adventure in my life started the moment I resolved to discover who I truly am. I use the word *truly* because I stopped settling with just anything life throws at me. I realized there was more to get from life. Throughout my

---

[11] https://www.politifact.com/factchecks/2019/sep/26/viral-image/nomarcus-aurelius-didnt-say-about-opinions-and-fa/

years as a young man in my twenties and thirties, self-doubt and hidden insecurities had a tight grip on my thoughts and behaviors, which resulted in poor decisions and outcomes for myself. My choices during that timeframe were based on a low mental construct about myself. I did not believe in who I was because of the hidden insecurities. I recall having a tough time trying to pass a few of my certification exams. I had convinced myself that I could not pass the exams because I was not a good test taker. Also, each time that I failed killed my self-esteem and self-confidence. Here I was able to complete my doctoral degree at the age of thirty and could not pass these certification exams. The shame and sense of failure hit a like a ton of bricks. Every day that I walked into work and looked into the faces of my colleagues who had their certifications, or when I sat at the executive table and was the only one without the certifications, created even greater insecurities about myself.

The turnaround occurred when I decided to adjust my lens to see myself as a success instead of a failure. I had to put in the work and dedicate time to studying the Word of God, praying, and test preparation to overcome some of the hidden mental challenges within. These challenges forced me to see myself in a new light because the day that I passed all of my certification exams was a glorious day. Adjusting your lens requires work and dedication to remain faithful and not to give up.

We all grew up acknowledging and approving of whatever people said to us, about us—what we could or couldn't do, who we are, who we are meant to be, and what we'll never become. How much of these things have you allowed to alter your focus and blur your self-image? We listened to what our parents, our teachers, that cool pal in school, and society had to say about us. These words left lasting impressions and vivid (but not always true) perceptions about our lives. From the cradle, starting in the home, we tend to find our true reflection in our parents' reality; then we move to the outer world, imitating what society stamps.

The way by which individuals view societal versus personal expectations is different and applies to how you might continue to adjust your lens.

Table 1: Societal vs. Personal

Societal Expectation	**Personal Expectation**
Students come to class prepared and ready to learn	I did come ready to learn, however; I choose to present it orally
Everyone works 40 hours per week	I like a varied schedule to achieve 40 hours per week
Homeownership is the best route to go	I cannot afford to purchase the home
Get married and stay married even it is a bad union	If I am not happy in the marriage, divorce is an option

Reflection

When you look at your life today, do you find a reflection of your ancestry? I mean, do you find yourself doing what Daddy likes, marrying the girl because she takes after Mommy, working the job because it's in the family line; are you reluctant to step out from behind the comfort of what's familiar into a risk of the unknown? And how much longer will you construct and define your life from an external standpoint? Isn't it time to calibrate your lens? 📖

What Does It Mean to Adjust Your Lens?

Usually, we wear a pair of glasses to aid and enhance the power and possibility of our eyesight. But it's also possible to get so used to wearing the same glasses that you become less aware of how much it helps your sight.

Not many people can quickly detect subtle defects in the quality and clarity of the images in front of their eyes. But why should anyone keep moving toward a blurred object? How much longer are you prepared to live or cope with a failing and false eyesight? How much further do you want to carry a wrong perception?

This is precisely the point I'm making. You need to know how to adjust your lens or get new glasses for a better, clearer, and brighter self-reflection and self-image. Fortunately, you don't have to be confused about how to do this. I'm not talking about twenty-one steps to change your life in twenty-four hours. Not a hopeless quick fix. Neither is it a doubtful chance of "Try this" from a self-help coach who has hardly helped himself.

Instead, adjusting your lens is simply one thing: looking intentionally within to see the One who created you. My friend, if this is *all* you get from this chapter, if you forget everything else, I've said, don't lose this powerful key. It's your access point to a greater life.

Many people would say that adjusting your lens is easy or can be switched around at any time. Take this into consideration. Think about when you've received any correspondence from a friend, neighbor, colleague, or boss. How you digest the contents of the message received varies from the lens its viewed through. So many times, we get the message wrong because of how we adjusted our lens. We read too much into how we perceive the tone, cadence, writing style, etc. From our lens, we've made judgments, our blood pressure has skyrocketed, and we sometimes act out of character due to misinterpreting the message. Remind yourself I must get this right now in adjusting my lens because it will cost me if done incorrectly.

As a leader in education and associate pastor for over 20 years, I've learned that how you respond to conflict or situation will determine the outcome. If approached negatively, the result will be negative, and no one wins from this position. However, if it comes from a positive position, it is more favorable to create a win-win. The adjustments you make in life and throughout this season will undoubtedly propel you to the next level of your greatness. Here are a few quick reference points to ask yourself as you adjust your lens to see the greater good within you and those around you.

- Pray for direction
- Mediate through deep breathing
- Ask yourself before I respond is this going to be beneficial or harmful
- Speak the truth in love and not condemn
- Take a quick break from a heated situation by walking away

Remember, you have been destined to be great. Also, be reminded that your lens may not change reality, but it will surely help you gain the right perception about reality. You have to keep this in mind as you examine your body as well as your situation.

After all, the reflection that stares back at you every morning as you get dressed and look into the mirror is one amazing creation of our heavenly Father. If only you can see every day, see how you are wonderfully and thoroughly made, your life will turn around for good.

The story of Nehemiah (Nehemiah 1-7:73) is a great demonstration of how to adjust your lens in the face of opposition effectively. God called Nehemiah to rebuild the wall.

As Nehemiah was working with the people to rebuild the wall in the temple in Ezra, opposition arose. Leaders of the people attempted to hinder Nehemiah's efforts through parody; however, the people had a strong desire to work despite their comments or negativity. When the leaders' words of negativity could not impact the builders from rebuilding, they decided to strike against Jerusalem. Amid the confusion, Nehemiah did not retreat; instead, he adjusted his lens to remain focused on the task of rebuilding the wall. Nehemiah leads his people to seek the heart of God through prayer and to arm themselves for battle. He reaffirmed God's vision for the wall and remain diligent in rebuilding the wall. Even as the threats grew, Nehemiah placed guards in critical areas to protect the builders. Please take a mental note from Nehemiah to do not get weary and well-doing because if you faint not, you will reap the reward. Nehemiah and the people's faithfulness allowed them to be victorious against their adversaries and the completion of rebuilding the wall.

You Need a Better Reflection for Life

Regardless of where you are in the spectrum of life, reflect and ask yourself, "Have I assessed the impact of my past experiences on my present perception about myself? Have I welcomed my future with soiled hands, or do I reject the hope yet to come due to my flawed experiences?" Just think about this as you read this story.

I read about the story of a young man who was born in an utmost challenging situation. He never knew who his father was, and this placed an obvious stigma on him among his peers. He lived under the haunting shadows of shame and daunting reproach until it eventually crippled what remained of his self-esteem. His reflection and perception about life gradually changed as he daily endured ridicule from kids in school who called him names.

It was so bad that he constantly had a feeling that someone was always there, staring at him and asking the same pathetic question, “Who is this boy’s father?” This made the young man spend a lot of time by himself, and he didn’t have any friends whatsoever.

One day, a pastor came to the town where he lived. Everyone talked about how wonderful this new pastor was. Every day, the boy thought of how pleasant it would be to meet with the new pastor so he could discover what the pastor had that made everyone talk about him so dearly. But sadly, that didn’t seem possible. The boy had no friends to hang with so they could reach him together, nor did anyone want to associate with him. Maybe the wonderful pastor is just like the rest of them—cold and unloving. He mused this over and over.

The young boy resolved to visit the church. He attended one of the services, and after hearing the pastor’s message, he too concluded that the pastor was amazing, and so he decided to keep going. But he came into the service a little late and left quite early, just to avoid talking to anyone each time.

One Sunday, he got so caught up with the sermon that he stayed back when it concluded. As he sat alone on his chair, he felt a hand on his shoulder, and when he turned around, it was the pastor standing next to him. The pastor asked, "What is your name? Whose son, are you?" Just as the boy was about to reply, the pastor continued by saying, "I know your Father; you are a child of God."

According to the boy, those words changed him. This young boy grew up to lead a responsible life in the reflection of the loving and heavenly Father, who stays forever. He was set free from the shadows of shame and daunting frustrations he suffered due to fatherlessness. He got a brand-new, unbreakable mirror; he got a better reflection. This boy stopped looking through the broken glasses of his broken past; he began to see through a brand-new lens.

Eventually, he became a beloved leader—a two-term governor of Tennessee. I'm sure you probably know him now. The young boy is Ben Hooper.

Only the moment you rediscover your true identity will your life begin to shift in the right direction. The moment you adjust your lens to gain a clearer image of who you are, you will no longer be a slave to your past. Neither will you be bound any longer to the unstable compass of your skewed reality. Indeed, **your greater** will start when your perception ends.

Understandably, adjusting your lens is not going to be a walk in the park; it might be a tall order for people who have always assessed their life through every other kind of mirror except through the reflection and the image of their maker. It's time for a much-needed reevaluation.

Fortunately, Ben Hooper learned at an early age that he was *not* a slave to circumstances, misfortunes, chaos, his harrowing past, or early predicaments. He quickly realized that he was a child of God, and this changed his life. Miraculously, Ben's anger, frustration, depression, wounds, hurts, and rejection were eliminated by the power of God's love. And no longer could people diminish his sense of dignity because he finally saw his true identity as a child of God.

Where Are You Running?

The story of Jonah is a perfect example that reflects a man who has been destined and designated for greatness beyond his wildest imagination wants to run from his purpose.

Jonah, a national influencer who chose to live like an ordinary man, did not quickly realize he was created for greater influence. Now the word of the LORD came unto Jonah the son of Amittai, saying, arise, go to Nineveh, that great city, and cry against it; for their wickedness is come up before me. But Jonah rose to flee unto Tarshish from the presence of the LORD and went down to Joppa, and he found a ship going to Tarshish: so he paid the fare thereof, and went down into it, to go with them unto Tarshish from the presence of the LORD (Jonah 1:1-3 KJV).

From this passage, you can know how a willful agenda of heaven is carried out. God wants to execute judgment over the land of Nineveh, and he looks around the whole earth seeking someone to send; his merciful eye catches Jonah. History has it that Jonah was a prophet, but not much was recorded about him before this time.

Perhaps the fact that Jonah had previously done no mighty works was one of the reasons he was reluctant to heed the call of God. Rather than run toward the great assignment, he ran away from it. If only Jonah had understood how significant his assignment was if he had known he didn't have to have performed many miracles as some major prophets had, perhaps his response would have been different.

Reflection

Have you too found yourself in such a situation? One where you ran as fast as you could from the purpose and great assignment that God has for you because you feel like you are unfit for the job, or because you think the task is too sacred for you? You probably think you're inadequately equipped for the engagement, so you settle for something less or easy. You forget that when God sends a man on an assignment, He goes with him. You forget the fact that you will always enjoy divine backing each time you yield to God.

The truth is that God knew you before He formed you, and He had your purpose in mind. And regardless of how the situation may be today, His purpose for your life is unchanging. So never focus on your surroundings, or whatever your reality relentlessly screams at you. Instead, adjust your lens and see your life and purpose as God sees you. See how great is the task God has placed ahead of you.

In Chapter 3 of Jonah, Nineveh is described as a great city that will take only three days for Jonah to journey to. But he threw away the instructions of God and headed for Tarshish. He tried to get away from performing God's assignment on his life. He did not realize the urgency and quickness that God placed on his assignment. Instead, Jonah only saw his inadequacy and allowed fear to convince his heart to disobey God.

But after he encountered the severity of God's assignment for him while on the boat, he determined to heed God's voice. And what was the effect of his mission when he finally surrendered to God?

So the people of Nineveh believed God, and proclaimed a fast, and put on sackcloth, from the greatest of them even to the least of them. For word came unto the king of Nineveh, and he arose from his throne, and he laid his robe from him, and covered him with sackcloth, and sat in ashes. And he caused it to be proclaimed and published through Nineveh by the decree of the king and his nobles, saying, let neither man nor beast, herd nor flock, taste anything: let them not feed, nor drink water: (Jonah 3:5-7 KJV)

For the first time in the history of mankind, a whole nation fasted to seek the mercy of God—even the beasts and animals in the land from the greatest to the least. Jonah became an all-time prophet whom God used for such mighty works, and his story is still being read several generations, today. It cannot be disputed that Jonah felt there was not a need for him and his mission at Nineveh. Jonah knew God would forgive the people of Nineveh for their sins as soon as he preached to them. But little did he know that both his assignment of preaching and the salvation of the people were relevant to God.

Reflection

You too must start to see the relevance of your purpose. Know that you are not an ordinary citizen merely with an obscure purpose. No! No matter how ordinary your assignment may seem in your eyes, understand that it is great in the sight of the LORD. And that is the perfect and only reality you should settle for. To understand more about how to unlock your purpose, let's try this exercise. Please take a sheet of paper and label it *"1-2-3" Purpose Activity*. The first thing you want to do is

1. Write a one-paragraph comprised of everything you are passionate about;

2. Add to declarative statements. An example is *I can see myself speaking in front of ten thousand people with confidence.* And
3. Write three personalized action statements or sentences of how you are going to work toward the two declarative statements. 📖

How Do I Begin to Adjust My Lens to See Myself as Christ Sees Me?

There is one essential action you must be willing to do to move to the next level of purpose. It is the gateway to falling in love with yourself and the One who created you. This is an active will of seeking the *truth*.

Truth has been used as a weapon of war instead of a tool for healing and freedom. People fight the truth, and they fight truthful people as well. That is why truthful and sincere people are hard to come by. People pave ways to escape the heat that rubs with truth by avoiding it. Looking at truth most people are not even true to themselves. Many people will not dare to be vulnerable, even while chatting with their doctors!

Many of us have a love/hate relationship with the truth. You are very selective about the truths you seek because your mental constructs have subconsciously falsified realities. You try so hard to not be vulnerable and open up unto the truth which is your essential reality. Instead, you revel in your present circumstance, esteeming it as what your life was meant to be like.

Left wounded and unwholesome, you rely on self to expose the cold facts about who you are. Cold because those facts not what is true, but what you have come to believe because of your inaccurate and biased sight.

However, it becomes impossible to get the correct answer because of our fractured state of mind. It is like you are trying to perform open-heart surgery without the proper credentials and tools because you continue to misdiagnose ourselves.

Therefore, you've created an alter ego identity, which counteracts the truth since we no longer have to dig deep or peel back the layers of truth. When you begin to peel back the layers of truth, the real journey of healing and self-reflection begins. You can uproot the fallacies that have perpetuated your mind and heart for so long. Right now, right here, you can adjust the lens to embrace self and a loving Savior.

How Confident Are You?

Daniel was a man who should not even be thought of as one wearing the medal of greatness. He was taken captive into Babylon when Jerusalem was besieged by Nebuchadnezzar, booted out to become a slave to the king. Being a slave in a strange land will break anyone.

It could affect his mentality and view of himself.

A slave has no ambition, no goal, no purpose anymore. If he ever had any dream in his mind, that dream disappears when he ceases to be free. All he can ever become is at the mercy of his master.

Freedom for Daniel was no longer an option. And there was no hope that he would ever regain liberty. His life was regimented, and so he could be justified for not entertaining the thought of greatness. He could as well think he was doomed for life and only rejoice if his master thought greatly of him. But something was interesting about Daniel.

Daniel made up his mind to eat and drink only what God had approved for his people to eat. And he asked the king's chief official for permission not to eat the food and wine served in the royal palace.

DANIEL 1:8 CEV

Daniel made up his mind not to defile himself in the land. Even though the opportunity for defilement was free and within reach, Daniel stood his ground. He refused to imprison his mind, but he hearkened to the liberty in his truth. His geographical location may have changed, but he maintained a perfect view of himself in the sight of God. And this informed all of his decisions in Babylon. He knew God wasn't seeing him as a slave or a captive. So he refused to act as such.

He kept his lens about his life rightly in place to see only the image of his Creator. His dedication to God landed him in the lions' den.

A decree was made not to pray to any god, only to the king. For Daniel, meant adjusting his lens to focus on the king. Daniel decided he would rather die than obey such a decree.

Well, he was found praying to God and was thrown into the lions' den. Who would expect that someone could stay alive in that situation? But interestingly, it happened. The next day, the king hurried to the den and called Daniel. To the king's amazement, Daniel replied from the pit amid the hungry lions,

My God hath sent his angel, and hath shut the lions' mouths, that they have not hurt me: forasmuch as before him innocence was found in me; and also before thee, O king, have I done no hurt.

DANIEL 6:22 KJV

Daniel's example shows that when you come into agreement with who you are in God, that mental picture moves your relationship from one filled with anxiety and cares to one of complete trust in him. The way he shows up for you begins to shift mountains on your behalf. He will quiet and remove the hollering voices in your mind that speak against you, that constantly seek your indulgence. Then you can start to speak with complete and total authority.

God has and holds the perfect lens. God holds the perfect lens to discovering your true identity, your actual reality. Which clarifying or magnifying lens you use doesn't matter because God has the patency of the right lens. And if you care, of course, you do care about seeing yourself in the right light; you opt for the lens that God only holds to see through it, your authentic reality.

Just like Jonah, you'll have to stand as one man to influence a nation as great as Nineveh. After just one sermon—Jonah's ordained assignment—the nation repented and turned to the LORD. But that did not happen until Jonah saw himself and his purpose from the lens of God, and he carried God's directive. He saw the relevance and urgency of his assignment and how it would deliver a falling nation.

Are You Set?

If you are willing to lay down old lenses to pick up a right and new one, then this is your chance. Take this moment to surrender your mind, heart, and soul to God, your Father. He knows you more than anyone, and the perfect lens anyone can see their life through exists with him.

He told Jeremiah,

❝

Before I formed you, I knew you.

JEREMIAH 1:5 NKJV

No one can claim an accurate knowledge and truth about you like God. Not you, not even your parents or teachers or mentors. He is not getting used to you like your spouse or your friends. You were first in his mind before he formed you with his hand. So come humbly to him.

Jesus said,

❝

Come and learn of me.

MATTHEW 11:29, KJV

In other words, he is always available if you desire to discover and learn about your truth. So are you in despair? Why not humbly cry out to the only God who can help you identify truth and set you on a path of success. He is always near; come boldly unto him.

In 2 Corinthians 3:18, we are told,

And we all, with unveiled face, beholding the glory of the LORD are being transformed into the same image from one degree of glory to another. For this comes from the LORD, who is the Spirit.

ESV

This implies that the closer you come to God and the more you keep your gaze on him and the mirror of His Word, the better you have clarity about who you are.

By this, your sight is sharpened as your old lens is exchanged for a newer and better one. Your reality then becomes what you see in Christ. You begin to reflect the image and likeness of Christ at every stage of your life. And as you adjust your lens through the insight of His Word, your daily decisions and perspective about life are altered, and you begin to take steps that will lead to your greatness.

Personal Commitment

Today, make up your mind to uncover and recover your true image and reflection in Christ. Never allow yourself to be defined by your past hurts, failures, self-esteem, and other mental constructs about yourself or by traumatic life experiences you once had. Neither should you let your environment or mental construct rob you of your greatness.

So come out of hiding and begin to walk radiantly in the liberty that Christ has made you free. Take charge, and live your life in the full reality of who God says you are. Because God says so, that is who you are.

And can you guess? God says you are perfect, and you are complete. "I am a masterpiece created by the Most High."

Affirmations

- I am fearfully and gorgeously made.
- I am ready to board the plane of truth and self-discovery in Christ.
- I am a champion, I am a warrior who is destined to receive a full all-access pass, and I cannot be stopped!

04

CHAPTER

Anchor in the Storm: Finding Stability in Christ

In order to realize the worth of the anchor,
we need to feel the stress of the storm.

CORRIE TEN BOOM

The anchor in any storm is contingent upon your location and position while in the storm. You can have a posture or position of fear or one rooted in the ground, just like an anchor in the sea. The anchor is the holding block that solidifies your understanding while everything around you may be falling. You've had to adjust your lens to anchor yourself while on your journey to **your greater**. The anchor is your lifeline. The anchor line represents strength; however, the line can only mean strength because of the metal it's connected to. If you think about it, the line by itself has minimal capability; however, when fused to the metal, the power is undeniable. In that same manner, God is saying if you would ground yourself in me, you will see the great benefits and rewards that come with it. In me, my promises are yeah and amen. This perspective helps you keep, sustain, and tend the dreams and seeds of greatness within you. And without stress, you find yourself living in the reality of what you have seen and discovered. Let's let the anchor ground you in truth, today!

Now, you must know that the path to greatness is not always like a highway free of potholes, bumps, or speed limits. However, the journey includes a mirror reflection that cannot be mimicked by anyone else. Many times, you attempt to slide on the expression or smile of someone else. The expression or smile doesn't fit because it was made for someone else and not you. You cannot assume someone's fight or expression or what they think of you, if you are not careful, you become the reflection of them that's why the reflection looking back at you feel uneasy or expressionless. The weight of anchor must be grounded well because it is the bridge for you to walk over to **your greater**. You will need to lean on the bridge in the transition process from time to time, and that is okay. Never be afraid of the bridge but embrace it with all sincerity. It is the key to unlocking the different phases of your life so that you can move your greater.

That means there will be moments of discouragement, times when it looks as though your cruise at 30,000 feet is a failed mission already, moments when all you see are impossibilities. There will be times when even your best efforts make no significant difference; times you probably will want to hold back and stay still. Also, seasons come in your life when the definition of failure becomes more real to you than the reality of your destiny. There are times when it seems like you are constantly in the midst of the storm with no hope of victory.

But the question is, how do you respond in such a trying time? I mean times when the difficult moments take root in your life and begin to bear fruits of impossibilities?

Before I go further, how does the anchor reflect itself in your life? How are you grounded within your anchor?

A boat cannot stay steady at a point. It has a natural tendency to move with the storm or in the direction of the water tide. But with an anchor, no matter how high or low the tide may be, regardless of how strong the storm may be, the boat remains steady and fixed where the sailor anchors it. Life brings good and hard times, but what sustains us is our anchor.

Do you also know that the strength of every tree against the wind is not its branches but its root? The root is an anchor of the tree, just like God is the anchor of everything he created. He sustains all things. And that includes your life! What we all withstand in life is indeed determined by the strength of our anchors.

Storms Test Faith

Tom Krause was awarded one of the highest achievements in music, the Bach Prize. His works are known throughout the world as a leading baritone, once said, "There are no failures, just experiences and your reactions to them."13 Do you believe this statement? Maybe you should think about it a little more. I know you are probably taking a look at the unpleasant situation right now, and you can't seem to call it anything but "failure." Well, I can understand. But failures are simply the building blocks and tools to cause a greater reaction toward your destiny.

It all depends on how you see your failures. Failure is not supposed to slow or stifle your progress toward you reaching **your greater**. But on the contrary, failure should be a part of the small stones if well-arranged well to become the building blocks to your greatness. Failures should become punch lines in your success story. As an inspirational author, Roy T. Bennett wrote, "Failure is a bend in the road, not the end of the road. Learn from failure and keep moving forward."[12]

---

[12] www.goodreads.com/quotes/7711461

However, there are times that life itself presents hardships and unpredictable timelines that weaken a believer's faith. You'll encounter situations that stare you in the face and make you question what you believe.

In the Bible, we read the story of a man that moved from being very great to being very poor all in one day.

This name has been discussed previously; however, the relevancy of his story is one to be admired and fits in many areas of your life. His name is Job. The man was faced with challenges. He didn't know the cause. He could not place his finger on the root of his calamity. A man that has it all going well for him and suddenly he lost his business and even his children in one day. Job himself was at death's door.

What do you think he should have done? Is that not enough for him to bite the dust? Based upon my perspective of Job's trails. But Job was never weak in faith. Listen! I hear you say quietly in your mind, "That was Job, do you think I can stand such a trying time?" But I want to tell you that you can! Your anchor is with you.

Carefully study the life of Job, and you will agree with me that the issues were just too much for one man. Even in the heart of these challenges, his wife asked him,

Why are you still holding on to your faith?

JOB 2:9 ERV

She never understood why a man beaten heavily by the storms of life would still stand on without giving in. She felt this sudden storm around him was too much; why not let go of the anchor?

Why not give up on your profession of faith when there is nothing physical to hold on to? When even your greatest confidants, people you think should stand by you, have deserted you, and you are all alone? This time is likely going to be the most unrealistic time to stand when you're left standing alone.

At such times, if you are not rooted and grounded in God, such unpleasant situations can cause you to challenge even the very nature and true essence of God. Because you probably look around, and the core existence of his presence can feel as if he's sometimes absent or not tangible.

The truth is, storms come to strengthen our faith, but rather, to sink our faith if we are not deeply rooted or planted in God's Word. I'm not referring to some day-to-day inconveniences like heavy traffic, a flat tire, or even a hassle at work. I mean difficulties that cause you to question God's goodness, such as a situation that makes you want to look into heaven in search of God just to be sure he is still there. Challenges such as illness, the death of a loved one, the threat of divorce in marriage, among others. Things that make it look as though God is fast asleep. Or does he care?

Amid such a situation, the stark reality of your displaced faith comes in to disrupt the flow and continuity of your faith. And this limits your view such that you no longer see yourselves and your life as meaningful anymore; neither do you see any value in yourselves. You feel absolutely rejected and dejected. This occurs when the storms of life can move you from one disappointment to another without your ability to hold yourself up. The pressure is too much. Your legs are buckling while the tears are running down your face. You see yourself slipping, about to fall, and no one is there to catch you. The mind and spirit attempt to speak to your subconscious, but the weight and gravity are unbearable. Each buckle of the knee is a running storyboard of each painful experience that cannot be erased.

Therefore, I ask, what storm around your life makes you question your faith and its value to you? Is it the circumstances that make you question your very existence, purpose, and value here on earth?

When All Strength Is Gone

There are times, of course, when you become so fixated on your issues that you simply forget who walks beside you or with you. All you see are the piles and loads of challenges around you. At such moments, your faith is questioned, and the strength you once had is now a distant reality trying to find its way home. All the bold steps you do take before are now absolutely impossible achievements.

When you feel you have put in a lot of effort, given your best shot to come out of the situation, but it seems all your attempts are like water flowing unhindered down the drain, I assure you that there *is* a way out. The four keys to rebuilding your strength and reconnecting your faith to reengage in ***truth*** are prayer, vision, intention, and a win-win attitude.

Appeal to Prayer

This first key is what lets you into a realm of no limitations. *Prayer* is the gatekeeper to attract God's attention toward your situation or circumstance. Prayer is a continuation of the self-commitment and affirmations you have engaged in throughout the book and will continue as it is a means to connect you, the reader with God's heart for your journey.

It is through prayer that God begins to whisper to you the needed changes to redirect your path. Prayer is not you simply talking to God about your problems and issues. No! It is having a genuine conversation with your Creator. He said in Isaiah 1:18 (KJV),

Come now, and let us reason together, saith the LORD.

ISAIAH 1:18 (KJV)

God wants you to share your hopes, dreams, and aspirations with him. You might be thinking, Well, he already knows. Yes, that's the point; he is all-knowing. However, he still wants to hear you open up in a way that is authentic and genuine.

God is a perfect gentleman; he is not going to force himself on you. He says,

Here I am! I stand at the door and knock. If you hear my voice and open the door, I will come in and eat with you. And you will eat with me.

REVELATIONS 3:20 ERV

For instance, Jesus was faced with so many thoughts and heaviness of heart as he approached the cross. Rather than make a decision that would jeopardize the plan of God, he simply went to God in prayer. As we learn in the Bible, an interesting thing happened as he prayed:

"

And there appeared an angel unto him from heaven, strengthening him.

LUKE 22:43 KJV

Don't tell more problems to people than you tell to God! I love what Christian author and pastor Max Lucado writes about prayer: "Our prayers may be awkward. Our attempts may be feeble. But since the power of prayer is in the one who hears it and not the one who says it, our prayers do make a difference." You must believe that your prayer makes a difference. Prayer brings a change and a renewal of strength. The power of your prayers settles all of your fears, doubts, and troubles of your unchanging anchor. Put to use, therefore, the power of fervent and effectual prayer in regaining your strength and passion.

Vision

Here is another powerful key to regaining and retaining your strength. What is *vision*? As you reflect on previous moments defining or redefining yourself, what are seeing as your vision toward **your greater**. Is it your ability to see what is invisible to many? In

Habakkuk 2:2, we are told,

Then the LORD answered me and said,
Record the vision and inscribe it on tablets,
that the one who reads it may run.

NASB

You can begin to design the vision of **your greater** by journaling about the key areas in your life that you want to enhance or increase. The areas must be specific to your right now, not necessarily your childhood dreams but rather in the things you want to achieve.

Vision is the roadmap to achieving **your greater**. Your vision must not only be conceptualized in your mind but written as well. There is an active response to move when you see it written down. And eventually, the vision becomes living when you begin to take active steps to achieve it. Nobody runs well without clarity of vision!

Your vision determines what you can or cannot do because it creates and maps your boundaries. It defines the limits of your possibilities. What you cannot see, you can never expect to actualize! Imagine, if you will, to instill the vision upon heart, you must make your vision a bracelet around your wrist, making it so clear to your sight that all your fears and limitations become irrelevant.

Intentional Movement

Intentional movement is the act of identifying measurable goals to reach your vision. These measurable goals are building steps to seeing the vision actualized in your life. Your intentionality must be specific toward the vision that is set before you. The connections you make and the people with whom you talk must lead you toward your purpose. Every step you take must be a deliberate and intentional move.

I press on to the goal for the upward call of God in Christ Jesus

PHIL 3:14 EHV

Think about Paul's statement here for some minutes. Did you discover anything about being intentional? *Press on to the goal!* Your steps must be taken in the direction of your goals and vision. It is important not to fight like one beating the air. Here are three steps to impact your vision for the next level movement to **your greater**.

- **SMART Goals**— to achieve success toward your vision, smart goals are warranted. SMART goals are measurable and specific. Many great leaders of the faith utilize smart goals as a part of the vision while giving direction and birth to vision.
- **Authentic Connections**—you cannot be afraid to connect with individuals in the areas of your vision. Reaching your next level of greatness requires making authentic connections. As you connect with these individuals, do not listen with the mindset of "give me," but instead, hear their stories.
- Ask direct and poignant questions about how they achieved their vision. Share a bit of your passion and story as you make these authentic connections. These connections will be your gatekeepers and door openers for you to achieve the vision.
- **Set Realistic Expectations**—Do not set unrealistic expectations for yourself. Realistic expectations are bite-size activities or goals to achieve your vision. You can set yourself up for failure by setting unrealistic expectations. An example of an unrealistic expectation: I am going to

make $500,000 during my first quarter of selling my new product line. Although it is a great long-term goal minus the first quarter by the fourth quarter, the short-term realistic expectation might be during the first quarter. I am going to invest in meeting five new authentic connections who can market and sell my product line to reach my fourth-quarter goal.

Win-Win Attitude

I have never seen anyone who talks defeat and ends up a victor. There will be times when it appears your goals and vision are not realistic and worth pursuing. You will be self-defeated, hurt, and ignored by others. However, these are the times when you must demonstrate a high level of faith and grit to see the vision come to pass. The first person who must believe in your vision is *you*!

Many times, the eyes that see your glorious destiny are few. But abandoning your vision for the sake of others will be disastrous. You cannot afford to listen to naysayers and those with negative perspectives.

Remember how Noah, who built the Ark, persevered to completion, and you see how God moved on his behalf because of his obedience. So through all the processes toward achieving your vision, maintaining a winning attitude, and keeping your head high above the waters of discouragement are paramount to achieving your greater.

Do You Believe Your True Image in Christ?

If you recall the reflection exercise in chapter 2, this is a continuation to solidify the belief of who you are becoming. You must keep the belief of who you are before you. Believing your true image in Christ is as important as knowing it! It is entirely a different ball game to believe what you know. Many have, for decades, made empty confessions of what they had never believed about themselves. I know that because of their response in times of troubles and challenges. Your response to challenges speaks a world about you. Have you seen a tea bag produce a sweat fragrance in cold water? No! You only know the content of a tea bag when it is put in hot water—believing in your ability to take God by His Word!

Note that regardless of the storm around your life, you are still fearfully and wonderfully made in the image of Christ. You are a masterpiece, a perfect image of the Most High God. You are the most prized possession of God, the greatest treasure in the sight of God than even the whole earth. You are so valuable that he let go of the only son he has just to redeem you from darkness and sorrow into the light and everlasting joy.

The truth is, it's one thing to see yourself in the image of Christ (that is, seeing yourself as God sees you), but another thing entirely to believe that view.

And until you believe your image in Christ even in the face of opposition, you may not have the boldness to walk in the reality of what you have seen.

By the way, talking about boldness, I am reminded of the story of an elephant. A man who was passing by a pasture filled with elephants looked a bit confused by what he saw.

Amid the parade of elephants, there was one unique elephant that was tied to a rope, there was no physical chains or fences holding the elephant hostage. All the elephants were moving freely and engaging in life as usual. But this particular elephant just seemed not to be interested; it looks very comfortable in its condition and doesn't look like it would make any attempt to join the rest.

At this point, the man pondered to himself, why isn't the elephant trying to break free from the rope? The elephant appeared hopeless and simply accepting of its fate.

Now let's pause right here; are you in the same condition? Stuck in a rut and cannot find your way out? Afraid to move because the enemy or the mental construct that you have built has kept you hostage, and you are not free to move? Yes! You agree that you like others, but also, there is a limiting mindset that keeps you at a spot telling you that you lack what it takes to do what others can do. You then confine yourself and your scope of influence to a spot. And just like the elephant, you accept your fate of a non-impactful and worthless existence.

Before we move on, let me tell you the rest of the story. Amazed by what he witnessed, the man went to the animal trainer nearby to ask why the elephant was not trying to break free. Why was it so comfortable in its confinement? Why was it not making any attempt to explore other possibilities beyond the radius of the rope?

The trainer gave an interesting reply. He explained that when the elephant was still a baby, much smaller in weight and size, the same and exact rope was used to contain it in that geographical area. During the elephant's baby years, the rope was an adequate size to hold it.

However, the baby elephant grew up in size and stature, with the ability to now break free. The full-grown and powerful elephant remained broken and tied to the rope. It was conditioned to accept its fate, still believing the rope had the strength and authority to hold it hostage and captive.

The man was amazed by the elephant's hesitance to respond by overpowering to break free from the rope. Now that it was fully grown, it had the power and strength to release itself from the rope. The elephant saw itself as an elephant, yet didn't believe the image. The elephant saw how powerfully built its muscles were but did not believe its muscles were strong enough to make any significant change. Therefore, it remained tied to the rope, at the same spot, accepting its fate.

Reflection

My friend, as you recognize your strength and anchor in Christ, take a moment to reflect on the greatness within you. Friend, are you tired of accepting mental constructs within your mind that continue to limit your capacity to achieve all that God has for you? Do you believe your view in Christ, as well as in the ability and potential for greatness that is deposited in you?

***

Anchor in Others

When the storms arise, who do you run to? Who is your anchor to keep you still? There are times that the silence acts like a ball-and-chain reaction in which knee-jerk decisions are made in haste and guilt and anxiety sets in, and finally, we look to others for validation and counsel. These are times when we just wish somebody was out there to beckon on us. The far cry for help seems hopeless and filled with despair.

Our resilience has shifted to self and away from the Problem Fixer.

One interesting scene happened in the journey of the Israelites from Egypt to the Promised Land. They got to a checkpoint, and Moses told God,

If you aren't going with us, please don't make us leave this place.

EXODUS 33:15 CEV

Moses was ready to abort the mission if God did not go with them. He knew there would be storms ahead, there would be challenges on the way, and so he didn't want to base their movement from that spot on the opinion and approval of others.

Let me quickly share this experience with you. Just recently, in my struggle and walk with Christ, I found myself lost in a wildness moment. I had to make an important decision about my next career opportunity. There were several offers on the table, and I was truly excited about what God was doing in my life. I began to consult respected friends about the offers to seek their advice.

Secretly, I hoped they would persuade or impact my decision-making. I remember seeking counsel from others before going to God in prayer about it first and allowing him to guide my footsteps. Throughout the process, I found myself stressed out, unable to sleep, and worried because I did not want to make the wrong decision.

The weight of the world was falling all around me because of the multiple decision that had to be made. You see, my decisions were impacting not only me but a family of five. Therefore, I did not want to miss the small voice of God whispering in my ear about the correct direction to take. How restful can you be on the opinion of others and not God?

God Wants to Be Your Anchor

Rather than rush into a decision because many people think it's the way out, sometimes it is essential to move to a quiet place away from the world and everyone in it so you can seek and hear from God about the next move or step in your journey to purpose and greater. And eventually, that was what I did. And after seeking God in my secret place in prayer, I was able to come to a decision and hear God about how to move to my next phase of purpose. You might be asking; how did you hear God's voice? God speaks in many different ways as you get in a position to listen to His voice. His voice is the inner voice from within. His voice is made tangible in dreams. His voice is realized in His Word. I was able to hear his voice by reading the Word of God and the stillness within my inner thoughts.

Holocaust survivor Corrie Ten Boom wrote, "There is no pit so deep that God's love is not deeper still."[13] In other words,

---

[13] https://christianhistoryinstitute.org/magazine/article/there-is-nopit-so-deep/

there is no challenge so strong that it is too much for God to handle. All other anchors will fail you amid the storm.

But faith in God is the strongest and surest anchor against any storm. Look at the promise God made in the book of Psalms:

"

The LORD directs the steps of the godly. He delights in every detail of their lives. Though they stumble, they will never fail, for the LORD holds them by the hand.

PSALMS 37: 23-24 NLT

I so love the fact that God is interested in every one of your steps. And again, I am dazzled that God Almighty, the surest anchor, said he is interested in every detail of your life! Do you believe that? Another important lesson here is that even though God is there, stumbling is inevitable. But you can be sure you will not fall because the LORD is your anchor; he holds you by the hand.

On your path to greatness, there will be storms, some heavy enough to make you want to turn back; strong enough to make you consider settling for where you are as your final destination. The LORD never promised we would not see storms in life (as a matter of fact, he has told us to expect trouble). But he has promised that he will be with us in the storm. Jesus said emphatically,

These things I have spoken unto you, that in me ye might have peace. In the world ye shall have tribulation: but be of good cheer; I have overcome the world

JOHN 16:33 KJV

That is, the staying power you need to hang in there in the face of despair is a firm faith in Jesus. He is the only anchor that can withstand all storms.

Understand, though, that some storms will make a mess of your expertise, storms that will let you know that relying on your intelligence or that of others around you is a waste of time.

There was once a time that Jesus and his disciples were in a boat on a mission to deliver a man who was fully possessed with legions of evil spirit. And as they journeyed toward that great deliverance, the wind and storm arose. It was not like the usual storm. Their boat was tossed to and fro and all efforts to still the boat proved futile. Peter and some of the disciples were fishermen, so they were experienced in facing the storms and knew how to keep the boat in position until they arrived at their destination. But this particular storm was beyond them.

And can you imagine that amid this storm, Jesus was fast asleep in one calm and comfortable corner in the same boat?

"

These And he was in the hinder part of the ship, asleep on a pillow: and they awake him, and say unto him, Master, carest thou not that we perish?

MARK 4:38 KJV

The disciples already envisaged that they would perish. But Jesus's hope was in God.

Finally, Trust God

One way to stay anchored to God is to trust him in all situations. Nobody sits on a seat without first trusting that the seat capable of bearing their weight. God wants you to be like Jesus in the fishing boat, saying, "Go to sleep." That is, in the midst of crisis and storm, while others are disturbed, express your boldness in God by staying seated. Take a nap, and rest assured that your anchor is not made of metal and rope that some kind of storm can break. Jehovah, the strongest of all, is your anchor.

There is an unexplainable peace in knowing that God is always there in times of trouble. The Bible says in Psalms 46:1 (ERV),

> *God is our protection and source of strength. He is always ready to help us in times of trouble.*
>
> PSALMS 46:1 (ERV)

He is ever-present to see you through. Maintain your faith in him.

Author Katie Kacvinsky once wrote, "All you need is one safe anchor to keep you grounded when the rest of your life spins out of control."[14] When everything is out of control, God is the

[14] https://www.goodreads.com/quotes/622602

one anchor; you need to stay still until you arrive at your greatness.

Personal Commitment

Today, make a personal commitment that no matter what situation in which you may find yourself, however unpleasant it may be, declare that you are an overcomer.

Affirmations

- I shall no longer lose my faith in challenges of life, but rather I will hold on to God as my anchor in the time of storm.
- I take a deep sleep like Jesus, knowing that God is at work in my life.
- I put my trust in God, and I'm not letting go of my faith in God.
- I affirm that God is working for my good.
- I believe the image of Christ, and I walk in the reality of my truth.
- I stay still in the arms of God and find rest in his love.
- I declare that I have God remains my only and safe anchor through the storm of life until I fulfill my God-given purpose.
- I smile at the storm, knowing that God is bearing me on his wings to my greater days.

05

CHAPTER

Plug In: Deepening Faith in Christ

Success, like happiness, cannot be pursued.
It comes only as a result of dedication.

VIKTOR FRANKL

Do you love flying on an airplane? What's your best part of flying? I've heard some people talk about the excitement at the moment when their plane is just about to take off as it speeds up to a thrilling rate of 160 miles per hour.

Yet to some other people, only a few things match up with the feeling of flying as high as 30,000 feet. They sit next to the window and look through it while the plane is moving in the sky, treasuring the beauty and glory within the colors of the clouds.

But have you met someone who looks forward to the time when visibility is poor and the cloud is dense? I bet there's no excitement when turbulence is felt in the air and anxiety begins to brew in the mind. Naturally, we just want to have a smooth, quiet, pressure- and panic-free flight until we arrive at our destination. Don't we?

How does this line up with our experience in the journey of life? Certainly, as much as we all want to have it easy throughout life, the landscape of our path is filled with hills and valleys. Therefore, the desire to get to our land of promise must be greater than our fear of the dangerous terrain.

The truth is, there are times when your faith can be displaced. Times when it seems like you never had faith in the first place. During this moment, your physical and spiritual selves are unable to connect as one. The unity of your spirit and mind is unbalanced, and the consequence of this displacement is a period of uncertainty. When you don't know what to believe anymore. Your spirit keeps assuring you of God's love, but your mind is bothered with all the challenges and uncertainties around. You ask yourself, "Can I still make it? This tunnel appears too dark; will I ever find the light? Is there hope that God's promise will come to pass?"

Well, it is important to understand that moving to the next level in your walk with God requires your faith to be tested: the core values that make up your essence will be challenged. In such moments, you need to have unwavering faith, which is a major key to plug in or in a simple term; stay connected to your reality as a child and servant of God. The Bible says on Habakkuk 2:4 (KJV)

... but the just shall live by his faith.

HABAKKUK 2:4 (KJV)

The Bible describes the story of Elijah and the prophet of Baal in 1 Kings chapter 18. To prove who the true God is, Elijah prayed down fire on a wet altar, and God responded. This was something the prophets of Baal could not do. As a result, Elijah slaughtered four hundred of the prophets. This he did to draw the heart of God's people from following other gods to serve the living God.

Can you imagine one man pulling such exploits by faith? However, in chapter 19, the queen of the land, Jezebel, sent a messenger to Elijah with a promise to execute him by the following day just as he did to the prophets of Baal.

You would expect that a man who confronted over four hundred men by faith would see the threat of a woman as nothing. But that was not the case. Elijah ran as fast as he could for about a day until he got to the wilderness. There, his only request was that God should take his life. Life was no longer meaningful and fulfilling to this great prophet of God. He felt it was over and that God was probably done.

Just like Elijah, you may come to a point where, in the looming eyes of despair, hope develops wings, and it's as though the walls are caving in around you. Or you may have a condition when situations around you make you feel like you're trying to find your way in a dark alley. In your mind, the walk feels like countless hours when, in reality, it has only been a few minutes. Anurag Prakash Ray once said, "Hard times are sometimes blessings in disguise. We do have to suffer, but in the end, it makes us stronger, better, and wise."[15] During hard times, we're retreat backwards, and time seems longer than needed; that's when you'll feel like throwing in the towel. The truth is, the rest of you feel the same.

What should be your response to situations that seem beyond your power? Should you give up and settle for less? Or

---

[15] https://www.wiseoldsayings.com/hard-times-quotes/

should you go around looking for help where shame is plenteous? I have discovered that rather than plug into God and His word, most people let their present circumstances dictate their every move.

They entertain fear, which makes them admit defeat when they could have navigated through the turbulence like a pilot in a dense cloud. From the example of Elijah above. Elijah knew how to connect and plug into God after sending down the rain, thereby validating the true God before the people. Also, he was bold enough to slaughter close to half a million men.

But when Elijah heard of the threat to kill him, his connection was shaken. He unplugged himself from the fountain of life. His focus shifted entirely from the ability of God to save him from the attempt against his life.

Just like Elijah, the pressures of life can have a monumental impact on you as you move to your greater. Remember, this is not the time to retreat or hide under the umbrella of fear. As a reminder, the umbrella serves as your protection while the rain is pouring down. Jesus says in Deuteronomy 31:6, "Be strong and courageous. Do not be afraid or terrified because of them, for the Lord your God goes with you; he will never leave you for forsake you".

Reflection

Have you ever given this a thought before: that any time we become fearful; we magnify our mountains to be larger than they are? We let the word of discouragement find footing in our hearts instead of plugging into God's Word for relief. Such fear drives us away from the pursuit of our greater. So despite your present circumstance, are you still plugged in? Or you are still looking for rain on a sunny day?

***

I remember the story of Job in the Bible. He's one of the few men that God referred to as perfect. Why? Because he was a man of integrity. He was wealthy and prosperous in all things. Although Job had great substance, he priced his relationship with God above all his treasures. His life was full of love and peace. Don't you think that is a good life, totally free of storms?

But something happened that destroyed Job's tranquil existence. In a day, he lost his children, business, and great wealth. A terrible tide rose against him to turn over his boat and sink his faith. Yet with the storm and other circumstances, instead of blaming God or losing faith, Job praised God. He plugged in! I mean, how could you praise God when all you have is gone, and even your life is nothing but hell on earth? At such juncture in life, will you also remain plugged in?

Meanwhile, Job's wife came to him and advised him to unplug from God. She believed it was better for him to die than experience such great pain. She said in effect, "Just pull the plug, and all these sufferings will end." But Job knew what to do when it seemed his world was caving in. He knew pulling the plug is just like shutting down his source of life and strength.

I want you to know that sometimes people tell you to unplug in the form of advice. They will show you several other options and places you can plug in to. You must be awake to know advice that is only packaged to unplug you from God. Have you been told to "unplug"? What is your response?

Understand that Job had the habit of plugging into God. How early you begin to plug in will determine your outcome and altitude, even in the most difficult situation. Plugging in, therefore, is a vital step or action toward your greatness. But the question is, are you ready to plug in to master your fate and realize your full potential in God? 📖

Hardship Is the Ingredient of Greatness

Frank A. Clark once said,

Hardships are necessary for growth so that we learn a greater dependence upon [GOD].

FRANK A. CLARK

The truth is, I cannot think of anyone who has experienced a level of success without first experiencing some level of hardship. Most great leaders in history once passed through the fire of tests and trials to emerge in their greater. Indeed, lasting success is always a sweaty adventure.

Most times, we don't know the intensity of the fire that gold endures so the best of its value can appear. Yet most people want to be valued without passing through the fire of trials. I always wonder why the same sun that melts the iced block also solidifies the clay. But then I realize that trails and circumstances of life are both great and small; what makes the difference is resilience so you can emerge refined and strong.

But know that hardships are executed for your growth and interdependence on a loving Savior who desires an authentic relationship with you. He is not watching you go through pains in life so you can be broken and drop off. No, but rather, he wants you to come to him and see him as the way out. It's therefore, your responsibility to look beyond what you can see in front of you, and draw near to your Creator.

Apostle Paul said in 2 Corinthians 4:17 (KJV),

These little troubles are getting us ready for an eternal glory that will make all our troubles seem like nothing.

2 CORINTHIANS 4:17 (KJV)

The truth is, the Christians in the early church went through skin-tear persecution. Some were beaten, stoned, and jailed, while others were even killed. But Paul described all these challenges as "little troubles," and a version of Scriptures refer to it as "light afflictions." This was not heavy for them because they were plugged in.

These people saw beyond the temporal challenges. They didn't look at the hardship, but rather, they looked through the obstacle and saw the weight of glory ahead. They saw the greater days ahead, and that view kept them plugged into God. They were not disturbed or moved by the situation around them. They kept seeing the prize! Pursue achieving the goals before you now with no settling back doing nothing.

Have you come across the inspiring experience of Kris Carr? She's a great leader who faced the uncertainty of her health after being diagnosed with stage IV cancer. You can only imagine the level of confusion and despair she felt after receiving this news.

Hardship will either propel you to move forward into **your greater** or peg you down to hopelessly accept your fate. The pebbles that life throws at you can either be used to build a wall that keeps you from moving forward or a bridge to cross over all impossibilities to **your greater**. Therefore, you must be willing to choose at the onset of any hardship. Either you trust God completely, or you stop pursuing a life of impact.

After hearing the prognosis of having a rare form of cancer in her liver and lungs, which was already at stage IV, Kris Carr decided to fight back. She didn't look down and wallow in self-pity. She changed her diet and looked into total wellness to regain her position and purpose. She further created a wellness website to encourage others to follow her same lifestyle and journey. She didn't allow her condition to dictate her choice. But instead, she saw a negative condition as an opportunity to move into her greater purpose.

Reflection

Are you confronted with a life-threatening situation? Have you already called-it-quits? Did you let the fear of the unknown cripple your pursuit of relevance and influence? Or perhaps you had unplugged from God long before disaster hit?

***

Interestingly, right from the creation of the world, man has developed the habit of disconnecting totally from God when things go wrong. Even in the Garden of Eden, Adam and Eve's reaction to God when they had committed high treason was proof that man usually seek solution in everything else except God.

However, God is gracious, and the fact that God still came to visit them knowing full well that they had eaten from the forbidden tree, is a sign that they were not totally out of alignment yet. His mercy still provided a place for them to plug in. Unfortunately, they pulled the plug.

What Would Be Your Choice?

Kris Carr's story points to how hardships can move you into **your greater** or live in a posture of unforgiveness, loneliness, and despair. Most people have died an untimely death because they chose to cave in to their problem rather than plug into a secured walk with God. Not many people are careful to see the blessing hidden and locked away in their trying time. All they seek is temporal ease.

Reflection

So what would be your choice? My question is, how often do you look at your hardships or obstacles and use them to your advantage? How often do you patiently wait for the sun to rise and brighten your heart after a long night of despair and uncertainty?

***

When you accept a relationship with your heavenly Father, you received the best gift. You know he created you in his image. If you think about it, the deposit of your greatness has already been given to you. He blew into you the breath of life, and you became a living being. That burst of air included sovereignty, love, grace, and above all, his DNA. Man is the king of God's creation. He made man rule and reign.

You will agree with me that God does not create junk. He is an excellent God with all shades of perfection.

The Bible says in James 1:17 (CEB),

Every good gift and every perfect gift is from above, and cometh down from the Father of lights, with whom is no variableness, neither shadow of turning.

JAMES 1:17 (CEB)

Isn't that awesome to know?

The Bible says ***every***, not some, not few, but every. I hope you know that if God is your Creator, then he cannot withhold anything good from you. You don't need to take a stroll outside of God to have the good things of life. Don't go all out searching everywhere for what comes only from God.

You are God's heir. Your inheritance is all encompassing, and it's accompanied by endless possibilities, opportunities, and *accountability*. Yes, that "a" word, accountability, is attached to it. According to the Cambridge Dictionary, accountability is "The fact of being responsible for what you do and able to get a satisfactory reason for it or the degree to which this happens."[16] You should know that all the multiple possibilities and opportunities you've received demand a high level of accountability to God.

Why accountability? God does not want irresponsible children. He wants his children to be people of high integrity and commitment; that's one way to stay plugged in.

Bear in mind that accountability is an extension of God's grace and mercy to assist you along the way to achieving **your greater**. You need to be reminded of this from time to time as you may get off track, not meeting your full potential. His love is deep and wide, and he wants what is best for you.

---

[16] https://dictionary.cambridge.org/dictionary/english/accountability

But in becoming all that God wants you to be, there will be challenges that will come like a roadblock on your way. No wonder Paul said in Romans 8:35 (KJV),

"

Who shall separate us from the love of God ...?

ROMANS 8:35 (KJV)

This goes to show that you have to deliberately connect your life into a close-knit relationship with God. Can you list your ***whats*** too? What are those things you see as things that could unplug you from the source? Look at them all in the face and tell them, Like Job, I know my redeemer lives, and I am resolved to stay plugged in.

Former American professional basketball player Michael Jordan once said, "I've missed more than 9000 shots in my career. I've lost almost 300 games. Twenty-six times, I've been trusted to take the game winning shot and missed. I've failed over and over and over again in my life. And that is why I succeed."[17] What a paradox! His success story was beautified by

[17] https://www.brainyquote.com/quotes/michael_jordan_127660

his down moments. It is no bad thing to stumble; staying there on the flow of regret is what you must never do.

No matter the height you wish to get to in life, the truth is that every great leader has to endure obstacles and face challenges at some points in their life. But you cannot allow those valley experiences to limit you. You must forge ahead to attain greater heights. The difference between average and great leaders is that the latter overcame hardships and improved themselves in the process. You can also do the same!

Whether you're someone's boss, an entrepreneur, a scientist, or a mentor, you have to look at your weakest moments as opportunities rather than limitations. You must learn how to be still and meditate deeply. Those who overcame such phases in their lives always stayed calm and collected. Do not rush into making decisions in your challenging moments. Make a choice! Stay positive and focus.

I'm sure you've heard about Bill Gates, who was once the richest man in the world. But do you also know that his company, Microsoft, was not his first attempt at success?

Bill's first company, Traf-O-Data (a device that could read traffic tapes and process the data), failed miserably. Then Gates and his partner, Paul Allen, tried to sell it, and even then, the product wouldn't work. At that point, they seriously contemplated admitting failure. All the sleepless nights and struggles seemed futile and useless.

But amid this obvious obstacle to success and wealth, they *tried again*. Gates and Allen didn't let the failure of Traf-O-Data stop them. Allen explained the impact of that failure this way: "Even though TrafO-Data wasn't a roaring success, it was seminal in preparing us to make Microsoft's first product a couple of years later."[18]

For this duo, failure was not final. It was the beginning of the journey. The fact is, obstacles and failures are just another step toward your ultimate destination or success. But your response and attitude determine if you'll be a winner or a loser.

A lot of great ideas have been buried because of an initial fear of failure. The question is not if you will experience adversity or hardship on your path to greatness, but how would you respond to it when it shows up? You can either allow it to discourage you, or you can turn it around to your advantage. What would be your choice? Don't forget; your choice must keep you plugged into God.

The Best Way to Succeed

Are you still looking for the best way to succeed? Clergyman Walter Martin once advised that "A key to

---

[18] https://medium.com/@thecoolestcool/don-t-stop-believin-a-look-atthe-founder-failures-that-came-before-unicorn-status-6498ce4ef374

strengthening spiritual muscles and enduring hardship is finding strength in the Word of God."[19]

I was once on a long quest for meaning and purpose. I sampled every option except for the right one. Finally, when I had exhausted all my energies, I turned to God, who said,

I am the way, the truth, and the life

JOHN 14:6 ERV

Indeed, true success can only be found in Jesus. My only fear is that many people make unnecessary adventures and come badly exhausted when they could have properly channeled their strength on that *one thing that is necessary*. Never neglect the compass to **your greater.**

---

[19] https://www.quotetab.com/quote/by-walter-martin/a-key-tostrengthening-spiritual-muscles-and-enduring-hardship-is-findingstrengt

How to Stay Plugged In to God

A professional baker will tell you that the dough must remain in the oven for a minimum number of hours, depending on its size. Any attempt to open the oven door or bring out the dough within that stipulated time deprives you of a perfect, well-formed cake. That's how it is with your connection to God. He desires to have you plugged into him always, not once in a while, until you fulfill your purpose. What are some practical ways to remain connected to God?

The Greater Equation

Let me start by showing you this perfect formula for **your greater**.

Surrender + Relationship = Your Greater!

Know that your heavenly Father wants nothing more than total surrender of your mind, body, and spirit to him. He said in Proverbs 23:26 (KJV),

My son, give me thine heart, and let thine eyes observe my ways.

PROVERBS 23:26 (KJV)

That's all that is needful.

He desires to have a place of rest in our hearts. He doesn't want to come like a visitor who is in today and out the next day. God doesn't want to check-in and out like a five-star hotel. He wants to dwell in you.

In surrendering to God, you are allowing him to fill you afresh with his love. The person you used to be is no longer active, and you embrace the newness of life. Like roses fully bloomed in spring, with each petal representing new birth, a new position, a new purpose, and newfound freedom to love as he loves are now yours.

While surrender is like the start of the journey, it doesn't end there. A relationship with God in truth and deed is also vital. Nothing excites God more than to have you close to him.

He created us for his pleasure. You can't achieve more by remaining far off. He wants you to draw closer. Jesus met Peter and said to him,

Follow me, and I will make you fishers of men

MATTHEW 4:19 (KJV)

Peter may not have arrived at **his greater** if he didn't follow Jesus and remained connected until death.

Peter surrendered all to Jesus, gave up his job and business, gave up his contact and associates, entered a lifelong relationship with Jesus, and this resulted in **his greater**.

So give it everything you've got, let go of those distractions and draw closer, and watch your success emerge like the morning sun.

Plug In to God's Love

God desires that you move from a semi-relationship with him to fully embracing his glory, his love, and his forgiveness. In her book *There You'll Find Me*, Jenny B. Jones asks, "Does your love reach this far, God? And if it extends to heaven and beyond ... why can't it seem to find me?" I have just a simple answer to these questions: because you're not plugged in! That's why the love of God seems like a fairy tale to you.

Amazingly, God's love *is* ever-present and available; you don't need to search for it, it seeks you, and you don't have to give anything to obtain it. God gave his only begotten son to have you. We gave nothing to God before he gave us his *all*. Do you believe in God's love?

Then embrace this love!

How Do You Embrace God's Love Fully?

Embrace means to accept something or someone willingly. It means to cherish and hold that something or someone as dear to your heart.

Christ wants nothing more than to embrace you with an overwhelming love like you have never experienced before. His love is genuine and full of truth. It is not based on your merit. You can never merit God's love. Love is his nature. And it is his response to you when you call on him during your trials.

We are told in the Bible,

But God commendeth his love toward us, in that, while we were yet sinners, Christ died for us men.

ROMANS 5:8, KJV

Christ didn't die for you because you were righteous. His love is unconditional, and if he didn't hate you then, he can't love you any less now. He died for your sake while you were still lost in sin. Let me put it this way: he died for you before you told your first lie. Before you were stained by sin, he already made provision for your cleansing.

However, Jesus said in John 14:15 (KJV),

If ye love me, keep my commandments.

JOHN 14:15 (KJV)

This clearly implies that proof of your love for God is by doing what he commands. Imagine being in love with someone, and your words mean nothing to the person? I bet you may back out of such a relationship pretty soon.

King David, a man after God's heart, said in Psalm 119:11(KJV),

Thy word have I hid in mine heart, that I might not sin against thee.

PSALM 119:11(KJV)

He wasn't set to joke with what God said. No wonder he moved from the lonely and dangerous backside of the desert, from following animals, and he emerged as king in Israel. **His greater** was incontestable. God used him as a standard for other kings after him. So, do you love God, obey His Word.

Fervent Prayers

Another way to stay plugged in is by consistent communication with God in prayer. Imagine a relationship where the couple does not communicate with each other. Communication remains the lifeline of any serious relationship. D. L. Moody once said,

Some people think God does not like to be troubled with our constant coming and asking. The way to trouble God is not to come at all.[20]

D. L. MOODY

[20] https://relevantmagazine.com/god/12-dl-moodys-most-profoundquotes-about-faith

So, talk to God continually, keep the communication line open. Nothing is more valuable than knowing what to do. God is all-knowing. Talk to him about your fears; he is a friend that sticks closer than a brother. Through prayers, he will begin to reveal deep things to you; you also receive direction to your greater and wonder how easy it can be.

Plug In Like Abraham

There was nothing enviable about Abraham before he met God. But God desired to take him through the path of greatness. But here was the condition: Abraham had to detach from his old life and plug into God.

God told,

Get thee out of thy country, and from thy kindred, and from thy father's house, unto a land that I will shew thee: And I will make of thee a great nation, and I will bless thee, and make thy name great; and thou shalt be a blessing: And I will bless them that bless thee, and curse him that curseth thee: and in thee shall all families of the earth be blessed.

GENESIS 12:1-3 KJV

As good as those promises of greatness sounded, it all depended on the next step by Abraham.

❝

So Abraham departed.

GENESIS 12:4 KJV

By that move, he came into an eternal relationship with God. God told him to walk before him, and he would be perfect. Abraham stayed plugged in until he finally became a friend of God:

❝

But thou, Israel, art my servant, Jacob whom I have chosen, the seed of Abraham, my friend.

ISAIAH 41:8 KJV

This man went from being a mere acquaintance to becoming a friend. He had such a strong relationship with God to the extent that God felt he could not proceed with his plans to destroy Sodom and Gomorrah without informing Abraham. The LORD said,

Shall I hide from Abraham what I am about to do?

GENESIS 18:17, ESV

What a connection!

Abraham practiced the formula of greater. He surrendered all and committed to a relationship with God. In the end,

Abraham was old, and well stricken in age: and the LORD had blessed Abraham in all things

---

GENESIS 24:1 KJV

He was indeed great, and even today, every child of God is connected to the blessing of Abraham through Jesus Christ.

Jesus said

Abide in me, and I in you. As the branch cannot bear fruit of itself, except it abides in the vine; no more can ye, except ye abide in me. I am the vine, ye are the branches: He that abideth in me, and I in him, the same bringeth forth much fruit: for without me ye can do nothing.

JOHN 15:4-5 KJV

This implies that your ability to bear the fruits of greatness is based on your connectivity to God. Stay plugged in so the nutrients needed to produce **your greater** can flow freely into your life. Disconnect from your wisdom, skills, and connections and draw closer to God.

Finally, the Bible says in 2 Corinthians, 3:18,

But we all, with open face beholding as in a glass the glory of the LORD, are changed into the same image from glory to glory, even as by the Spirit of the LORD.

2 CORINTHIANS, 3:18

In other words, as you develop an unwavering connection to God, you start reflecting on his glory, and **your greater** becomes revealed to all.

Personal Commitment

Today, make a personal commitment to fix your gaze on Jesus. You now understand that hardship is part of the ingredient for greatness. So rather than looking at the obstacles that may shift your faith, plug into God: declare that you will always see what he says about you, not doubting His Word.

Affirmations

- I believe that Jesus died to give me a better life.
- I know he didn't consider my ways before stretching forth his hand of mercy and grace. From now, I smile at every storm and obstacle. I take all the pebbles that life throws at me as a step to my greater achievement. I refuse to allow my faith to be displaced anymore.
- I remain strong in faith. I walk into a deeper and more meaningful relationship with God. I am complete in him.
- I move from faith to faith and not from faith to doubt.
- My life is plugged into the Most High God, and I stay connected to him as the only channel to my greater.

06

CHAPTER

Go Deeper: Moving Closer to Your Greater

And the remnant that is escaped of the house of Judah shall again take root downward, and bear fruit upward.

ISAIAH 37:31

Have you heard of the Chinese bamboo tree? It is quite unlike any other plant, besides the fact that it also requires sunlight, good soil, and water to grow. But the distinguishing feature of this tree is in the way it grows.

In the first year, the Chinese bamboo tree is planted, there are no apparent signs of growth. In fact, up until its fifth year, nothing will be seen above the soil's surface. Most unlearned farmers get frustrated over such an unfruitful venture. In such a condition, it looks like all efforts to grow the tree have failed.

However, in the fifth year, something mind-blowing occurs. The Chinese bamboo tree begins to grow, and in only six weeks, it reaches about 80 feet. Doesn't this sound a little bit surreal? Yet this is pure fact.

Now, the catch here is, that the Chinese bamboo tree wasn't inactive for four years. On the contrary, it was growing underground. All those years, it was establishing a reliable root system that would sponsor its external growth for the duration of its life. Such underground growth is necessary for longevity. The tree had to go deeper to reach its **greater**.

Success Is Built on Foundations

Likewise, this growth principle applies to those who desire success in life. The saying "Nothing good comes easy" has been overused, but its meaning still rings true. To get to **your greater**, you must be ready to go deeper like the Chinese bamboo tree. You must be willing to pursue your dreams patiently, learn to rise from failure, overcome setbacks, and persevere despite challenges. In so doing, you would establish a solid root system or foundation that can sustain success.

Many people aim to be in the limelight, but not many understand that success in life is a process. It starts from a humble beginning to a glorified summit. And ignoring the process is like boxing the air. We might be enthusiastic about getting to our greater but might end up missing the target.

As much as you want to have greater achievements, greater happiness, and greater fulfillment, you need to realize one thing. Greatness comes through a process because you must build the success you desire. And you know nothing can be built without an established foundation.

Therefore, you must be willing to let God take you through the process of deepening your roots. Your deeper-season is where you build solid foundations for greatness. It's the key to getting to **your greater** season of manifestation and breakthrough.

David Went Deeper to Achieve Greater

The Bible says,

"

So David reigned over all Israel, and he administered justice and equity to all his people

1 CHRONICLES 18:14

He was showing David to be a remarkable leader. Much is known about the epic battle between little David and the Gath giant, but little is known about David's deeper-season. We tend to focus on his conquest and reign over Israel and miss the little details that point to the root of his success.

On the battlefield, the godless Philistine, Goliath, kept defying God and the army of Israel for forty days. Meanwhile, God searched the entire Israeli army for a defendant, but unfortunately, there was none. By divine providence, David showed up on the battle scene and volunteered to confront the giant.

King Saul offered David his armor, but David politely declined. He had no clue what to do with it, and it weighed him down. God hadn't sharpened him that way. During his seasons of going deep with God, he hadn't encountered armors and swords, but stones, sheep, lions, and bears.

All those years, David had been underground like the Chinese bamboo tree; God had taught him to trust only in God. His roots were firmly in God, so he showed up with greater confidence, ready to walk into the battle arena with nothing but a sling and a pouch of smooth stones. What happened next turned the battle in Israel's favor. David sank his stone into Goliath's skull, and the giant fell to the ground, dead.

God regarded David as a man after his own heart. In other words, he was God's favorite. However, God is not partial but endears utterly those who endear him. David was a man who was entirely given to deepening his roots in God. He allowed God to sharpen him and proved to be an extraordinary battle-ax.

David Positioned Himself for God to Find

And when he had removed him, he raised up David to be their king, *of whom he testified* and said,

I have found in David, the son of Jesse a man after my heart, who will do all my will.

ACTS 13:22 (KJV)

The Bible said that God raised David to be king in the above text. Now, isn't that interesting? When exactly did God raise him? For years, he wasn't known. Neither was he regarded in his family. Do you see that David was just like the Chinese bamboo tree that had been growing for four years, yet nobody thought it was making progress? Indeed, all those years David spent time with the sheep, God was raising him underground to be king. Yes, David was deepening his roots and sharpening his leadership skills.

Has God hidden you for some time? Do you feel like no one knows you, or you're not making progress like others? Just like David, God is raising you. This is why you shouldn't be jealous when others appear more successful than you? God is more interested in your roots because once you're deeply established in him and your life's purpose, nothing can stop **your greater**.

God said about David,

❝

I have found in David, the son of Jesse a man after my heart, who will do all my will.

ACTS 13:22

I want you to note the word ***found***. The little shepherd boy was always singing and praising God in the field. His parents didn't consider him worthy of a crown. But God's searching eye caught young David preparing for the throne.

While other young men were doing something different, David kept honing his battle skills and developing the heart of a wise leader. He mastered the use of slings, learned how to care for and protect helpless sheep, and took on the responsibility. But more importantly, he learned the art of pleasing God. Little did he know that he was being prepared for enthronement.

Everything you experience in your pursuit of greatness should draw you closer to God. You must go to him to take you through the process. David had to watch his flock at night, fight off wild animals, and wrestle lambs from the mouth of lions. His experience as a shepherd must have been one of great sacrifice and love for animals that couldn't reciprocate. Still, amid all this, his roots were going in deeper to make him rise to **his greater**.

Young David was found worthy because he had yielded to the building process of success. God saw his commitment to going deeper. What about you? Where are you on God's radar? If God should scan through the earth for a man or woman after his own heart, would he find you?

David's glory began to manifest the day God singled him out for the kingly anointing above his elder brothers and even Saul. This is because David had been faithful in the secret place. He had given himself to being sharpened and prepared by God. He had grown underground; therefore, it was time for public manifestation.

Queen Esther's Preparation

Just like a tree with its roots deep into the ground, those roots may not be perceivable to others. Still, undeniably, the process of greatness starts with that. You need faith and perseverance to press through and come out victorious during this period.

Have you read the story of the young Hebrew girl Esther? A girl who rose from obscurity and nothingness into greatness. If you haven't, that's fine. Let's get cozy as you learn about how she moved from her lonely preparation and moved to the palace as a queen.

In the third year of his reign, King Ahasuerus had a banquet that lasted for seven days, and on the last day, he sent for Queen Vashti to display her beauty before the people. But she refused the king's request. The king became furious and ordered that Vashti's position as a queen be given to another.

So the king declared months of preparation that would produce the choice queen. All the qualified virgins in the land of Persia were brought to the king's palace to be adequately prepared for the position of a queen.

If an earthly king would need adequate preparation for those he desired to lift into the great height of being a queen of Persia, how much more does the King of kings need? Do you think he wouldn't take his time to prepare you adequately for **your greater**?

God desires to bring you into realms of greatness, but that will prove abortive without ample preparation. Mordecai, full of wisdom and expectations for Esther, decided to enroll her in the contest. Now, Esther was not the only one ready to take a walk down the path of greatness.

But the question is, who is ready to be thoroughly trained and cultured for the palace among them? Having a desire to be great is never enough. Wishful thinking and positive confessions are good but not sufficient to translate you into your realm of greatness. The reason is that if wishes were horses, even the beggars would ride. To become significant in the journey of life, growing deeper in your days of preparation is paramount.

Another vital thing to note here was that Esther was never a free ranger.

❝

And let the king appoint officers in all the provinces of his kingdom, that they may gather together all the fair young virgins unto Shushan the palace, to the house of the women, unto the custody of Hege the king's chamberlain, keeper of the women; and let their things for purification be given them:

ESTHER 2:3 KJV

Her preparation seemingly confined her to a place— the palace. And she was charged under a tutor—the chamberlain, who was to give her instructions and leading. Also, your preparation season will be colored with restrictions of freedom and expression—but that is part of the deal for greatness! God will place you under men and women who will guide and guard you through this period.

All the ladies had to undergo beauty treatments for twelve months. They had to be bathed in oil of myrrh for the first six months and another six in sweet odors ointments before they could appear before the king. The time of your preparation is not forever—it is timebound!

Think about John the Baptist. Even though he was born to herald the coming of the Messiah, he had to wait until the time appointed by the Father. Remember, the China bamboo tree does not grow deep forever. It will eventually send forth its branches of greatness.

Now, when the king requested that the maidens be brought before him after the twelve-month of preparation, all the maidens were to be given anything they would fit their **greater**. So, when it was Esther's turn to appear before the king, she displayed a quality the other ladies failed to learn in their preparation stage.

Esther became an orphan at an early age and was raised by her uncle. She saw the hard part of life even at a young age but grew to become a beautiful woman. Her season of grooming began in that little house of Uncle Mordecai. She learned obedience and submission under her uncle's guardianship.

You may wonder how I came to that conclusion. Now, look at what Esther did, which no other maiden did before appearing before the king.

Now when the turn of Esther, the daughter of Abihail the uncle of Mordecai, who had taken her for his daughter, was come to go in unto the king, ***she required nothing but what Hegai the king's chamberlain****, the keeper of the women,* ***appointed****. And Esther obtained favour in the sight of all them that looked upon her*

ESTHER 2:15 KJV

Esther learned obedience and was content with what was given her by the king's chamberlain. She wasn't all out to satisfy herself. You see, the period of preparation is a time to learn and unlearn behavior fitting for **your greater**. Before you appear in your greatness, you must be well prepared with godly values and virtues that will keep you there unshakable!

After Esther's ride into **her greater**, her years of preparation were now going to produce a fruit of greatness that would satisfy and preserve a whole nation—the Jews. There was a man dear to the king called Haman. He commanded respect, and people bowed at his feet except for Mordecai (Esther's uncle) because he was a Jew. Haman took offense and made the king sign a decree to wipe out the Jews in the land of Persia.

In times of trouble, your response will be what you've learned and internalized in your time of preparation. So what did Esther do to save her people? She immediately ordered,

Go, gather together all the Jews that are present in Shushan, and fast ye for me, and neither eat nor drink three days, night or day: I also and my maidens will fast likewise; and so will I go in unto the king, which is not according to the law: and if I perish, I perish.

ESTHER 4:16 KJV

Esther had to act fast as things had taken a turn for the worse when she heard Haman had ordered gallows to be made for the hanging of Mordecai. Esther sent word through her uncle to the Jews to be on three-day fasting and prayer. Esther has learned the power of prayer under the tutelage of her uncle—Mordechai. However, appearing before the king was death if not summoned.

She managed to convince the king and Haman to attend a banquet, which she made for them twice. On the second day of the feast, she opened up to them, saying she was a Jew, asking the king not to kill her people, and telling the king about Haman's plans to kill Mordecai. The king became furious upon hearing the information, and he ordered the hanging of Haman. The king gave the Jews the right to defend themselves against anyone trying to kill them, and Mordecai was made prime minister.

Earlier on, I talked about God preparing people to represent him on earth. The story above is one of God's representatives. God put Esther through the incubation period. She was just a maiden and only took care of her uncle Mordecai, she had no experience in being a queen, and looking at her background, you'd think she wouldn't have stood a chance to be the queen, but just like the other ladies, she allowed herself to be prepared.

We saw in that the preparation that she was made to bathe in sweet-smelling oils and perfumes for a year. She had been prepared for the position of a queen; she was assigned seven servants. What did she know about having people at her disposal? However, she had to conform. She had to learn to be in a better posture, how to speak publicly, and many other things that are to be done to walk in the shoes of a queen.

Now, what was the manifestation of Esther's preparation? She led her people to victory, and they defeated those against them. So, you see where God planned her to be determined by the peculiarity of her test and preparation. The whole process brought a more confident, and dynamic personality out of her. She stood as a leader of her people, made plans, and executed them with success.

With this, you'll understand that God takes time to prepare us for the position we are to fill. Your position may not be a queen's position; it might be the position you desire. It may be your desire to be a great leader, a business sage, a minister, or a politician. Still, you need to realize that it takes time of preparation for God to place you in such an estimable position.

The Ultimate Elevation

Author Corrie Ten Boom writes, "Every experience God gives us, every person He puts in our lives is the perfect preparation for the future that only he can see."[21]

Even though God wasn't mentioned throughout Queen Esther's story, it has so much evidence of God's plan. God set her on a path to be elevated, and she became queen of the Land of Persia, but that wasn't all. God knew what would happen, and he placed her in that position to succeed. Esther's faith was tried. She could have easily turned a blind eye and cared less about her people perishing, but she worked with God, and she conquered.

The time of preparation made Esther conform to the position she was in. It made a more courageous person out of her. She learned to trust and depend on God even more. In the Book of Esther 4:16, she submitted to God's preparation plan,

---

[21] https://www.goodreads.com/quotes/94188-this-is-what-the-past-isfor-every-experience-god

and that gave her the ultimate elevation. The elevation isn't only in her position as the queen but also in her heart and mind. You have to keep in mind that you are undergoing preparation, so;

a. First, you have to allow God to lead you to wherever or whoever he wants to lead you to. Everything that God brings on your path has a purpose; set your mind on finding that purpose.
b. Second, just as Queen Esther didn't allow leaving her comfort zone to affect her, so shouldn't you. It's not easy to conform to a new way of life, but you have to leave your comfort zone to get anything done.
c. You have to be confident and courageous because you are bound to take risks, just as Queen Esther did. She took a chance to make a request of the king, saying, "If I perish, I perish." These risks, believe it or not, take you a step higher. Whether it comes out good or bad, you learn either way.

Just as God refined the heart of Esther to become that of a queen, your preparation may be happening right now. Maybe you're not in that elevated position yet because your heart isn't ready, and God can see when you aren't ready for something like that. Going through the preparation helps you to act smart, rationally, intelligently with God's wisdom even when the devil tries to bring you a temptation. You show the devil you are God's faithful representative!

Jesus Christ Had the Deepest Roots

Jesus Christ is our ultimate example. Apostle Peter said,

Christ has been made an example for us that we should follow in His steps

1PETER 2:21

The ultimate prize Jesus got for going through the deeper-season and then being sharpened for three years until his death was his enthronement at the right hand of the father.

Thirty Years of Growing Underground

We cannot possibly overemphasize the remarkable impact of Christ's three-year ministry on earth. Why? Because it took him thirty years to prepare for it. During all of those years, he was establishing the systems for his work on earth.

Jesus Himself, when He began [His ministry], was about thirty years of age
....

LUKE 3:23 AMP

Those thirty years enriched Jesus with the uncanny ability to handle the issues of life with wisdom. His doctrine and judgment on the issues of money, marriage, law, godliness, and more were final. He had been imbued with the Holy Ghost anointing in the secret place. He had fixed his roots deeply in God.

We learn in the Bible that just before he started his ministry, Jesus was led to the wilderness by the Spirit of God to be tempted by the devil (Matthew 4:1). Stemming from his absolute obedience, Jesus had a robust wilderness experience that strengthened him against Satan's temptations. Here, he was sharpened to be an effective battle-ax for God.

Jesus Was Submissive

Worthy of note is the exceptional humility portrayed by Jesus Christ in his preparation days. Even though He was God, he submitted it to his early parents.

In Luke 2:51 ESV, the Bible says,

"

And he went down with them and came to Nazareth and was submissive to them. And his mother treasured up all these things in her heart."

....

LUKE 2:51 ESV

"

And Jesus increased in wisdom and stature and favour with God and man.

LUKE 2:51 ESV

During the period Jesus grew underground, He learned certain positive behaviors that enabled him to manage success in the days of **his greater**. Indeed, the deeper-season when you are being prepared by God is essential to your rising. It is time to develop the spirit of meekness and responsibility. Jesus was God, but he chose the highway of humility and submitted to his parents.

Although your deeper-season is a period where God works on you, it should not be done in absolute isolation. You know that even if the Chinese bamboo tree grew underground for four years, it was still being watered and tended. In the same way, give yourself over completely to the Holy Spirit. Yet you need to submit to a worthy mentor/disciple. It will build in you a sense of responsibility. And by divine counsel, you will grow your way to **your greater**.

Jesus Was Focused

Amid distractions, Jesus's eyes were fixed on the ***joy set before him***—the throne that was prepared for him. His preparation period on earth lasted thirty-three years, but not without overwhelming difficulties and challenges engineered by Satan to veer him off course. If Jesus wasn't focused, he would have traded his eternal throne for a temporal one.

Take a look at John 6:15 (KJV):

When Jesus, therefore, perceived that they would come and take him by force, to make him a king, he departed again into a mountain himself alone.

JOHN 6:15 (KJV)

Jesus wasn't enticed by what he saw. He knew his deeper-season hadn't ended. He knew there were still lessons to learn and processes to go through. Yet how many of us would be like Jesus? If you were allowed to skip the process of building genuine, long-lasting success, will you reject it like Jesus?

How focused are you? Do you still compromise for fleeting pleasures? Jesus was tempted by Satan, who wanted to give him a false kingdom; afterward, his people offered him another kingdom. You must understand that temptations will come to take you out of the process, but you have to be focused. Just imagine a farmer growing a Chinese bamboo tree, after a year of seeing no visible signs of growth, decides to unearth the seed. Won't that be a huge loss?

Therefore, you mustn't be distracted by pain or pleasure, frustration, or excitement; keep your eyes on your goal—on **your greater**.

Isolation for Glorification

Jesus Christ was a lover of the secret place. He was addicted to being alone with God. That was one of the secrets of his ministerial success. His faith was ever-increasing because he tarried long with the Giver of Life. Jesus's glorious transformation was a result of his perpetual attendance in God's presence.

God is fond of isolating his chosen ones so that he can elevate them. In essence, God will set you apart to elevate you before your ultimate elevation. Do not take your period of preparation lightly. Spend time alone with God, your Father. With him, all things are possible.

Jesus's Glorification

The manifold manifestations of Christ's glory span both earth and heaven. Jesus was a man of isolation. His faithfulness in the secret place paved the way for divine blessings upon him in many ways; here are four.

1. **Anointing for healing:** Now when the sun was setting, all they that had any sick with divers' diseases brought them unto him; and he laid his hands on every one of them, and healed them (Luke 4:40, KJV).
2. **Angelic visitations:** The premier angelic encounter of Jesus was after the wilderness experience, which fueled his victory over Satan's onslaught. Also, the appearance of saintly beings on the Mount of transfiguration directly resulted from Christ's submission to the process. God saw that he was committed to his deeper-season and decided to begin the preparations for the final lap.
3. **Fulfillment of purpose:** Life is a waste without purpose. You aren't truly alive until you have a purpose. Jesus had one purpose: to save us from sin. Due to his prior commitment to his preparation process, He was

strengthened by the Spirit of God to fulfill his God-sent mission.

4. **Enthronement at God's right hand:** Going through the process of preparation comes with great benefits. For Jesus, his entire season of going deeper in God and learning obedience culminated in his ascension. Indeed, He went deeper, down to the depths of hell, to get to **his greater**.

Celebrate the Small Wins: David's Testimonies

At the beginning of this chapter, we saw that the Chinese bamboo tree has to grow underground for four years to ensure its longevity when it begins to expand outward. Likewise, when you go deeper into God and go through the necessary processes that make for success, you will have something that ensures your longevity.

Testimonies

Testimonies are not just stories. They are the strength on which you rise to **your greater**. David could confront Goliath because he had a testimony of God's repeated deliverance, so he said,

The LORD that delivered me out of the paw of the lion, and out of the paw of the bear, he will deliver me out of the hand of this Philistine ...

1 SAMUEL 17:37 KJV

It was his guarantee of longevity. David knew he wouldn't die on the battlefield because of his testimony.

Indeed, a man's testimony is the signature of God's grace upon him. Besides, your testimony signifies God's revelation to you and through you. David's testimony was resounding. He had gathered enough warfare experience during his deeper-season. Therefore, he was quick to win the battle—rise to **his greater**—even before it began.

God's secret dealings with David included a complete course on warfare. God prepared in a specific way for a glorious manifestation. What about you, friend? How rich is your preparation for success? Can you say you're going through the process of being sharpened by God? The depth you reach in this season determines the height of your success. Your roots need to go deep until you contact your testimonies.

Finally, everyone God prepared and sharpened went ahead to do great things in the kingdom. They faced hard times, and, at a point, it looked like the pain of the process would swallow them up, but they pulled through. Let their story inspire you to go through the process also. The journey to **your greater** is not upward, but downward as you grow your roots in God. And whenever you're feeling down, just remember, God is raising you.

Personal Commitment

Now that you know that success has foundations, you must go deeper to get to **your greater** commit yourself to the process. It will not be a walk in the park, but it's going to be worthwhile. Set your heart afresh to seek God in secret, and walk in his ways; determine in your heart to persevere no matter the difficulties you face on your way up. Also, ask for the grace to resist the distractions.

Affirmations

- I am greater than the things my natural mind can conceive.
- I will dig deep into God to find nourishment.
- Like gold, I will pass through the fire to be refined.
- God has given me the strength to go through the process required for my success.
- No matter how long it takes, I will remain faithful and reach for the stars until my greater comes.

07

CHAPTER

It's Time to Redefine Your Greater

The world needs your greatness. Your time is now.

BRODIE WHITNEY

I feel so excited to know that you've made it to the last chapter of this book. You've made it this far on your journey to greatness. You've made it this far in the process of adopting a ***greater now*** mentality as a must-have mindset for success in life. So regardless of where you are and who you are, it's your time and your turn to be great.

I challenge you to turn on your inner ears and listen to the roll call—that voice asking, "Who's next to be great?" I challenge you to respond by saying, "Me, of course!" When the question is, "Who's next on the railroad of greatness?" you'll respond with, "I am."

When is the time for your greatness to manifest on a bigger stage and better clime? I dare you to say, "If not, now, when? If not here, where? If not me, then *who?*"

Friend, get ready! No more mini-mindedness, no more low-level thoughts—it's time to benefit from **your greater** mentality! It's time to profit from the growth mindset and dump that fixed mindset. It's time to reach beyond the status quo and break the bounds to your greater now.

Now is the time to believe in yourself. It's time to take off your shoes, roll up your sleeves, and launch into the deep to reclaim your treasure. This chapter is a celebratory one. You are now getting ready to take an active stance and position yourself toward **your greater**.

Put God First

Life can become so busy, competitive, and even chaotic. These are times when your priorities will be tested. Yet there's an anchor that holds in the storms of life. And that is keeping your eyes on God, the only constant.

As soon as I reassessed my priorities, I quickly realized that my **greater** was to be found in alignment with my Creator. We all want to feel loved and valued. God is the only one who truly loves you despite all your flaws, insecurities, frustrations, and doubts.

God said in Jeremiah 31:3 (CEV),

I will always love you; that's why I've been so patient and kind.

JEREMIAH 31:3 (CEV)

And, the moment I realized that God had declared his unwavering, unchanging, and unrepentant love for me. It changed everything. God took all of my continuous negative thoughts and transformed my stinking thinking into a reality of perseverance and hope. Indeed, the truth is that our source of inner strength does not come from us but our heavenly Father.

Yet I Needed Clarity

Writing is a divine gift to us. It provides clarity, direction, and energy. More than a thousand fleeting thoughts, a written word can light up the fire in our hearts. But my question is, what have you done with what you've seen? Do you know what it means to capture and crystallize your ideas? Have you ever taken one moment to write them down? You ask, "Is it necessary to write down what I see?" Absolutely, yes, it is.

A lot of people have lost sight of where God is taking them to because they fail to write it down.

"

And the LORD answered me, and said, write the vision, and make it plain upon tables, that he may run that readeth it

HABAKKUK 2:2 KJV

And the first thing that God looked out for was his preparedness to note the things He would say to him.

The prophet's expectations were high, yet God didn't allow him to depart from God's presence without writing down the things he was told.

You see, the process of writing it down leads us to take a running leap of faith to believe that we are much greater than our current circumstances. God emphasized this while discussing with Habakkuk. God says that anyone who reads about His greatness plan for them would be energized to run until it is fulfilled.

Power comes in many forms; however, the critical source of power is defined by our inner strength or the will to push ourselves in the midst of doubt, fear, guilt, or feelings of inadequacy.

Plainly written visions and goals help us to fix our gaze on the greatness that lies ahead of us in the face of apparent impossibilities. Hence the need to be sure you're writing down what God is showing you.

It's your turn and your time to be great, but do you have writings or journals that remind you of where you are going and prevent you from settling where you are? We all need a form of a compass in our hands that guides our minds as we navigate the path to **greater**. So, if you want thinking aid, mental focus, and guidance for decisions, then *write down your vision make it plain.* You have a responsibility to keep yourself on track to your glorious destination. Don't neglect it!

Think Greatness to Become Great!

British philosophical writer James Allen wrote, "A man can only rise, conquer, and achieve by lifting his thoughts. He can only remain weak, and abject, and miserable by refusing to lift his thoughts."[22] This goes to show that life largely answers to mentality. Your reality begins with your thought pattern. What you think about determines what you believe and what you believe ultimately determines how you act.

For as he thinketh in his heart, so is he ...

PROVERBS 23:7 KJV

For instance, if you think you will fail in an assignment that you thought makes you start feeling like a failure already. And before long, you will begin to act like a failure until you ultimately fail.

Most great men will tell you that the first step to greatness is the mindset to be great. You are in your season of greatness,

[22] https://www.amazon.com/As-Man-Thinketh-Complete-Original/ dp/1250309336

your greatness is now; therefore, no more little thinking but greatness thinking. Just as we are told in Philippians 4:8,

❛❛

*You should think of honorable things, maintain a pure, lovely, and excellent mental construct to emerge at **your greater**.*

PHILIPPIANS 4:8

Systems Thinking

One of the most prominent theories today that impact how we believe and think is known through *systems thinking*. Environmentalist Donella Meadows explained it as "a set of related components that work together in a particular environment to perform whatever functions are required to achieve the system's objective."[23] Many imagine systems thinking as linear; however, it is circular in motion with every aspect of interconnectedness.

[23] Perkin, Neil, Agile Transformation: Structures, Processes and Mindsets for the Digital Age (London, New York: Kogan Page, 2019), 55.

This implies that diving into **your greater** requires a total mindset change as you move to an interconnected relationship with your heavenly Father. You were created to be in harmony and constant fellowship with God. The interconnected relationship promotes a greater dependency on him.

Hence, you can make an informed decision to follow up daily without fear or doubt. This is because God has not given you a spirit of fear but of love and power and a sound mind. With this connection, you are confident that your greatness is secured once your life is aligned with God and His Word.

You will have to shift your thinking to move into **your greater**. You may not become what you cannot conceive in your mind. However, let me share with you a few active steps to shift your thinking to move into **your greater**.

1. **Visualization.** Your sight is a major element in your journey to greatness. Because it is always unto you in life as far as your eyes can see, this step requires seeing yourself in the position of your greatness. It is important to understand how you see yourself because this will challenge you to move into the next phase of your purpose. Therefore, see yourself become what you are destined to be. For instance, Moses came to God and started complaining about the challenges on his path to greatness, how Pharaoh seemed like an immovable roadblock to the fulfillment of his purpose in life. Rather

than empathize with his self-pitying condition, on the contrary, God simply told Moses,

See, I have made thee a god to Pharaoh

EXODUS 7:1 KJV

In other words, you are greater than all these limitations, so wake up and see your God-level greatness.

2. **Reflection.** This requires that you take an introspective look into **your greater** and begin writing down the activities to achieve **your greater**. What are the mediocre steps you need to stop? What are the relationships you have to terminate? What should be your daily schedule and routine that will lead to **your greater**?
3. You see, the things you do within your twenty-four hours will determine your success in life. So rewrite your to-do list, and prioritize the activities that will lead to **your greater**.
4. **Determined Mindset.** The truth is that there will be oppositions and naysayers; life will present you with cogent reasons to give up and let go of your dive to **your greater**. And this is the difference between great men

and mediocre ones. Many people shy away from the slighted scare, barrier, or contention on their way. But you must understand that your willpower and inner strength to succeed have to be greater than your potential. This implies that you must be resilient to achieve **your greater**. But also remember: the inner strength you need to stand strong and determined to succeed can only be drawn from a deep-seated connection with your heavenly Father.

These three attributes will lead you to move in a different position and mental perspective as you obtain **your greater**. And because you are connected to God and His Word, you begin to take accurate and precise steps that are correct and in alignment with his plan and purpose for your life.

Fix Your Focus on Your Greater

Even as you think about **your greater**, there are times when your thought wanders away from your path to greatness. Motivational speaker Eric Thomas writes, "Don't think about what can happen in a month. Don't think about what can happen in a year. Just focus on the next twenty-four hours in front of you and do what you can to get closer to where you want to be."[24] You

---

[24] https://buildinganest.co/motivational-start-budget-quotes/

know what this means; stay focused on your destination even in your mind.

I am reminded of a dove, a bird that represents the significance of Christ and the Holy Spirit. The eye of a dove is a perfect description of focus. Because of the narrow shape of its head, a dove can focus on a single object at a time. Its eyes are like telescopes, and can only focus on one direction at a time. That is how we should be on our path to our greater. There will be distractions, no doubt, but I learned something from Jesus: he endured the cross and also despised the shame. Did you see that? There are things that are attractive but also distracting. At one time, they wanted to make Jesus king, but he despised it.

Right now, it is time to focus only on your greater and nothing else. As the Bible tells us,

The light of the body is the eye: therefore, when thine eye is single, thy whole body also is full of light; but when thine eye is evil, thy body also is full of darkness

---

LUKE 11:34 KJV

There has never been a time more important than now. Set aside time or even reset if necessary. Allow your sight to engage in a more impactful way than before. The eye of the LORD will lead you to all truth regarding **your greater**. In John 16:13, Jesus says *the Holy Spirit will lead us into all truth*. But He will only lead when you are ready to follow only His instruction and directives.

It is Christ who has a singular focus for His sheep, and more specifically for you.

For I know the plans that I have you declares the LORD, plans to prosper you with a future and a hope.

JEREMIAH 29:11 KJV

Christ has already declared that He has intentional plans for your life. He only asks that you have a singular focus, just like the dove. God has His eyes on you right now. He wants you to move into **your greater** now.

Yes, you may not be where you thought you would be at this point in your life. So, push the reset button and begin again. It is never too late to start over. If you think about when Christ died for our sins, He simply set the reset button so we could live in purpose. You have overcomplicated the matter by overthinking and overanalyzing everything.

No Limits, No Boundaries

As you focus on **your greater**, you'll encounter self-limiting thoughts. Thoughts that say you can't achieve it, thoughts that try to box you in and keep you small. Thoughts that try to redirect your focus from **your greater** to something else. You are tempted to keep your thoughts on what you can't do and what seems impossible. But as the motivational speaker and author Wayne Dyer puts it, "The only limits you have are the limits you believe."[25]

You must be ready to move to pass the limits and boundaries. You are now ready to soar higher to achieve all that God has for you. There are no limits or boundaries that can limit your thinking because now you are in position. That is, you are willing to achieve greatness despite the limitations around. Get ready to check out of the room of impossibility that has crippled a lot of great potential within you.

I am reminded of Harriet Tubman, a woman who looked at her day's civil and social injustice and wrote a new narrative that is still told today. She led many people to freedom, including

[25] https://in.pinterest.com/pin/239253798937569365/

her family and friends. Her pursuit of seeing herself free one day became the heart anthem running through her veins that fueled a movement on the Underground Railroad to freedom.

Tubman pushed despite obstacles, naysayers, and others who did not believe in the movement. She never lost a slave on their journey to freedom. Her tenacity and drive aided her in blocking out distractions to achieve the goal. Just like Tubman, you have to block out the noises and distractions that attempt to hinder you from achieving **your greater**.

The truth limitations should not define you. The backbone of your strength must be rooted in a greater dependency to succeed. You must be willing to fight the good fight of faith to **your greater**. At this point, you can no longer escape the reality of planning and setting daily targets to achieve **your greater**. I can recall many days of feeling hopeless that my greater would not manifest. This was due to the limitation and internal conversations about not feeling enough.

My thoughts became so consuming that I almost had a breakdown. The pressure of not achieving a certain status and not obtaining my goals got the best of me. One day it all hit with my emotions colliding and resulting in a deep reflection moment with tears falling. All I kept asking myself was, "How did I get here."

Quickly, I realized I was trying to do it all in my strength without removing the barriers of self-doubt and the chronic naysayers in my head. If this is you right now, drop every thought of doubt, fear, worry, and inability, and realize that **your greater** potential is wrapped up in Christ. And that was what I did; I had started to rewrite the vision of greatness I once had. I reset the daily task and asked my heavenly Father to forgive me for leaning on my strength.

You see, no one can limit you but you. Yes, I repeat, *no one*. Not your teacher, not your family, not your partner, not even your colleague. Jim Carrey once said, "Maybe other people will try to limit me, but I don't limit myself."[26] You have all it takes to overcome and break every limit, and it begins now. Ask yourself what your excuses are. What is stopping you from taking that bold, giant step? What is holding you back from taking a high leap? Guess what limitations and those fears have tried to stop others in the past, yet they pulled through. Now it's your turn; will you allow fear to stop you from advancing to **your greater**?

Finally, ...

Our greatest treasure is to know the will of God for our lives. That is where **your greater** is. Where are you planted? Where has God positioned you? This will help you overcome all distractions as you advance to **your greater**. We can't allow any hindrance to distract you from moving into **your greater**. You

---

[26] https://everydaypower.com/jim-carrey-quotes/

are worth it, and God is ready and willing to walk alongside as you run full speed ahead to **your greater**.

Personal Commitment

Start taking the steps to greatness from now. Solomon said,

He that considers the cloud will not sow

ECCLESIASTES 1:40, TRANS

So start despite unfavorable prevailing circumstances. The rest of your life is the best of your life. Start by taking steps toward greatness daily, develop yourself daily, subject yourself to continuous improvement. Make greatness your only choice. And you will get there. It's your time; nothing must stop you. You must get there.

Starting now, commit to seeking God like never before; commit to developing a deep connection with God. Take the limits off your mind. See yourself the way God sees you. Look beyond where you are right now. It's not later but now. God is ready to propel you into **your greater**; you are the only factor in question. Make up your mind to think rightly. And tell yourself, "It's not only my time, but it's also my turn to be great."

Affirmations

- I agree with God that all things are now set for my greatness.
- I bear the fruit of greatness as God has destined me to be.
- I am no longer drawing back. I will take the necessary steps to achieve my greater now. 🕛 I move daily in the direction of my greater.
- I have all it takes to reach the peak, with God's help.
- I'm arriving at my God-ordained destination.
  My greater is now!

About The Author

Dr. Derrick Love is a career educator with over 18 years of serving in higher education and K-12 public education. He also has extensive experience in pastoral ministry. Dr. Love has numerous publications to his name and continues to serve in the local church. He aspires to bring out the best in people through living Christian principles to their greater. He is married to an amazing woman, and they have three energetic children.

Dedication

I want to dedicate this book to my amazing wife, who allows me to walk in my purpose daily. And to my three energetic children who keep me young, relevant, and fresh. I've struggled to find my footprint throughout the years, and now it is becoming more apparent as I move into my purpose. Thank you to all my family and friends, and may God continue to bless and keep you.

About Kharis Publishing

Kharis Publishing, an imprint of Kharis Media LLC, is a leading Christian and inspirational book publisher based in Aurora, Chicago metropolitan area, Illinois. Kharis' dual mission is to give voice to under-represented writers (including women and first-time authors) and equip orphans in developing countries with literacy tools. That is why, for each book sold, the publisher channels some of the proceeds into providing books and computers for orphanages in developing countries, so that these kids may learn to read, dream, and grow. For a limited time, Kharis Publishing is accepting unsolicited queries for nonfiction (Christian, self-help, memoirs, business, health and wellness) from qualified leaders, professionals, pastors, and ministers. Learn more at: About Us - Kharis Publishing - Accepting Manuscript

Reflection Journal

Date: ________________

Reflection Journal

Date: ________________

Reflection Journal

Date: ________________

Reflection Journal

Date: ________________

Reflection Journal

Date: ________________

Reflection Journal

Date: ________________

Reflection Journal

Date: ________________

Reflection Journal

Date: ________________

Reflection Journal

Date: ________________

Reflection Journal

Date: ________________